# DEBATING MEDIEVAL NATURAL LAW

# Debating Medieval Natural Law

---

A SURVEY

RICCARDO SACCENTI

*University of Notre Dame Press*

*Notre Dame, Indiana*

University of Notre Dame Press
Notre Dame, Indiana 46556
www.undpress.nd.edu

Library of Congress Cataloging-in-Publication Data
Names: Saccenti, Riccardo, author.
Title: Debating medieval natural law : a survey / Riccardo Saccenti.
Description: Notre Dame : University of Notre Dame Press, 2016. |
Includes bibliographical references and index.
Identifiers: LCCN 2016028707 (print) | LCCN 2016032539 (ebook) | ISBN
9780268100407 (hardcover : alk. paper) | ISBN 0268100403 (hardcover :
alk. paper) | ISBN 9780268100421 (pdf) | ISBN 9780268100438 (epub)
Subjects: LCSH: Natural law. | Law, Medieval—Influence.
Classification: LCC K460 .S23 2016 (print) | LCC K460 (ebook) |
DDC 340/.112—dc23
LC record available at https://lccn.loc.gov/2016028707

*To Donatella,*
*for our love,*

*and to Matilde Maria,*
*for her future*

# CONTENTS

# ACKNOWLEDGMENTS

I am in debt to the many people who supported the research and writing of this book, although of course I alone am responsible for its contents. This book is the first product of a research project concerning the relation between the historical development of the idea of natural law and the magisterium of the church. The Fondazione per le Scienze Religiose Giovanni XXIII in Bologna has supported this research since 2012. Alberto Melloni, director of the Fondazione, took special interest in my research, offering invaluable suggestions and comments. I would like to express my deep gratitude for his support and his trust in my work. At the Fondazione my interest in natural law was shared by Cinzia Sulas, who always offered keen observations during our discussions. I am grateful to her for this exchange of ideas and for her kindness.

On several occasions, I presented and discussed the contents of this book with all my colleagues at the Fondazione in Bologna. With some of them I had the opportunity to discuss my research on a daily basis, and I profited greatly from their friendly notes and comments. I would like to thank especially Patrizio Foresta, Dino Buzzetti and Davide Dainese, as well as Pier Cesare Bori, who passed away before I completed my research project.

Several friends and colleagues read the manuscript and offered wise suggestions. I am grateful to Gianfranco Fioravanti, Christian Moevs, Timothy Noone, Constant Mews and Francesco Borghesi. I also would like to thank Julia Schneider for her essential and patient revision of the English text and Frederick Lauritzen for his stylistic advice. The anonymous reviewers who read the text during the peer review process offered useful comments, for which I would like to thank them. I also offer my gratitude to the staff of the University of Notre Dame Press for their care and assistance as I prepared the manuscript for publication.

Finally I would like to thank all the members of my family, who supported me during the months I spent studying the issue of medieval natural law. In particular, the love and patience of my wife, Donatella, and our little daughter, Matilde Maria, made it possible for me to complete this work. I dedicate this book to them.

# PREFACE

"Io, che son la più trista, / son suora a la tua madre, e son Drittura, / povera, vedi, a fama e a cintura" (For I, in sorrow first, / Am Justice, and my sister gave you birth— / Though as you see, my clothes are of small worth).[1] In these verses, Dante Alighieri offers an allegorical presentation of Justice and uses the image of three women to characterize three kinds of justice, namely, what medieval authors called natural law, or "drittura" (*ius naturale*), law of nations (*ius gentium*), and civil law (*ius civile*). According to Dante, these kinds of *ius* are deeply connected as *ius naturale* is the mother of *ius gentium* and the grandmother of *ius civile*.[2]

An ancient interpretation of Dante's thought juxtaposes *Tre donne* to Chaco's words in *Inferno* 6.73: "Giusti son due, e non vi sono intesi" (Two are just, and no one heeds them).[3] According to interpreters of the *Divine Comedy* such as Jacopo della Lana, the Anonymous Selmiano, and Pietro Alighieri, the two "giusti" no longer respected in Florence are those of law and custom, *ius* and *mores*, or those of divine and human law, *fas* (*ius divinum et naturale*) and *ius gentium sive humanum*.[4] The reference here is to the opening pages of Gratian's *Decretum*, where the author, quoting Isidore of Seville, explains that human nature is ruled by customs and laws and that "natural law" (*ius naturale*) is contained in the laws of Moses and in the Gospel. In fact, this law of nature corresponds to the Golden Rule of Matthew 7:12: "All things therefore whatsoever you would that men should do to you, do you also to them. For this is the law and the prophets."[5]

The Florentine poet and his ancient commentators seem to have in mind a conceptual framework composed of *ius naturale* or "drittura," *ius gentium*, *ius civile*, the Golden Rule, and divine will. Using this "conceptual map," Dante places himself within a long and complex intellectual tradition to which several legists and decretists, theologians, and philosophers belong. Starting with Gratian, several authors have dealt with the way in which *ius naturale* could be considered the basis of both the legal and moral orders. These authors developed an understanding of this peculiar kind of *ius* that encompassed its very plurality: it is a rule, a moral principle, a power proper to human nature, an instinct. *Ius naturale* became a crucial topic in medieval culture, and its history reflects the developments and turns in political, economic, and religious life. Harold Berman, Paolo Prodi, and other historians have offered detailed analyses pointing out the place that medieval discussions of *ius naturale* occupied in the historical process. Following the last decades of the eleventh century, radical changes occurred in the cultural, political, and ecclesiastical structures and institutions of Latin Europe.[6]

Many scholars have devoted themselves to the study of the medieval history of the ideas of natural law and natural rights. This literature grew rapidly in the twentieth century, especially after World War II, when "human rights" became a focus of moral and legal cultures. The aim of this literature was and continues to be to define the features of the evolution of these ideas looking back to the medieval roots of modern "rights" doctrine. In its presentation and debate of the various interpretations of the medieval development of *ius naturale* and *lex naturalis*, this literature has deepened our understanding of the intellectual background against which Dante's allegorical representation of natural law stands.

Evaluating the main results of this lengthy research requires clarifying concepts and ideas, stressing continuities and discontinuities, and delineating the limits of medieval ideas of natural law and natural rights and their contemporary heir, human rights. This book offers a critical review of the way in which we look at the crucial conclusions that scholars reached in their inquiries. My goal is to establish the *status quaestionis* of the historical debate and demonstrate key differences among scholars. At the same time I show how several apparently opposing opinions and interpretations are in fact complementary. I examine the works of the most important contemporary scholars, presenting a portrait of medieval *ius natu-rale* and *lex naturalis* that attempts to uncover both highlights and areas of contemporary research still in shadow, the unsolved prob-lems, the aspects hitherto ignored of this portrait of the woman who shows up to Dante with the name "Drittura."

# INTRODUCTION
## Questions and Research

One of the main questions in the study of natural rights and natural law is when these concepts first came into use in the modern period. Originally *ius naturale* was synonymous with *lex naturalis*, an objective rule or prescription. At a particular point in time, *ius naturale* began to refer also, or more strictly, to a specific right belonging to each human being. The distinction between *lex* as objective rule and *ius* as subjective right marks the beginning of a new language and is a basic feature of modern rights theories. The history of these concepts involves not only the discovery of a crucial turning point in the history of ideas. To establish the "birth" of the modern idea of natural rights means also to determine the way in which it happened. Is there a specific discontinuity in the history of ideas, a moment after which the legal, moral, and political lexicon radically changed? Or is there a longer and more complex process, during which natural rights language shifted from its ancient meaning to our modern understanding?

Some authors stress that the origin of the modern notion of natural rights has to be linked to the specific features of the modern age; for others, it is to be found in medieval legal and political thought.[1] Twentieth-century historians and philosophers, as well as jurists and theologians who have focused on natural law and natural rights, adopt different points of view according to the cultural and intellectual contingencies in which they live and work. In this light,

1

an evaluation of their interpretations of the medieval doctrines of natural law and natural rights requires general remarks on the different cultural "seasons" and circumstances in which these authors studied and worked.

The rise of totalitarianism and the dramatic experience of World War II created a crisis for the positivist legal tradition and the political order it had produced since the middle of the nineteenth century. In this context, several intellectuals and philosophers elaborated the idea of "human rights," that is, natural individual rights proper to every human being, which the state through its laws must protect and support. Many thinkers debated the philosophical status of human rights, particularly after approval of the 1948 United Nations Universal Declaration of Human Rights. The idea that there could be rights that limit political power because they are "natural," that is, not established by any authority but simply recognized by human reason as proper to human nature, questioned the basic assumptions of legal positivism. The consequence was that thinkers who came from a positivist culture started to moderate their radical denial of the existence of any kind of natural legal principle. Herbert Lionel Adolphus Hart, for example, in his famous article, "Are There Any Natural Rights?," suggests that the existence of at least one basic natural right can be admitted: the equal right of all men to be free.[2]

Within this cultural framework, historians focused on the origins and roots of contemporary natural rights and looked back to the medieval notions of natural law and natural rights. In addition, one must remember that the discourse on *ius naturae* and *lex naturae* was quite commonly classified as part of the history of ideas. Ever since the publication of Arthur O. Lovejoy's *The Great Chain of Being* (1936), this kind of historical study has been much questioned and debated, as also in relation to the development of discourse on natural law and natural rights.[3] Several scholars, particularly those belonging to the Anglo-Saxon intellectual milieu, have devoted increasing attention to defining the epistemological criteria for evaluating the features and development of a concept in different moments of its history.[4] These two elements are crucial also for studies concerning the place of natural law and natural rights from the eleventh to the fifteenth century. These studies have to be placed alongside another cultural development in the first half of the twentieth century, namely, the new interest of Catholic intellectuals in the Middle Ages and the debate about the foundations of modern political discourse.

## The "Master" of Natural Law

The increasing interest in medieval civilization, which Pope Leo XIII stimulated and supported, led to a series of historical and philological studies that aimed to present the great texts of Christian medieval thought.[5] Among the subjects of interest was natural law, which in the decades around the turn of the twentieth century was a topic of debate and confrontation between Catholic and secular cultures. The Catholic interest in natural law and natural rights of the Middle Ages had a significant turning point in the 1920s and 1930s. It is in these decades, when the Catholic Church faced a complex situation with respect to totalitarian regimes, that fresh attention was given to the issues of *lex naturalis* and *ius naturale* and to the question of their mutual relationship.[6] Several authors, such as the philosopher Jacques Maritain and the Dominican medievalist Marie-Dominique Chenu, moved from the idea of a return to a medieval Christian civilization to that of the construction of a "new Christianity."[7] This philosophical and theological orientation was supported by a new historical approach to the evaluation of medieval philosophy and theology.

In 1922 Martin Grabmann published an essay offering a general overview of the development of the doctrines of natural law and natural rights between the ages of Gratian and Thomas Aquinas.[8] Through a detailed series of quotations from the writings of twelfth- and thirteenth-century canonists and theologians, the German scholar showed how complex and clearly articulated were the roots of Aquinas's doctrine of *ius naturale*. Since Gratian the medieval discourse on "Naturrecht" engaged both canonists and theologians, who melded the Roman legal and philosophical culture and the heritage of the Church Fathers. According to Grabmann, various authors, including Peter Lombard, Magister Gandulphus, Stephen of Tournai, Praepositinus, Stephen Langton, and Philip the Chancellor, contributed to the debate that prepared the way for the season of great scholasticism.[9]

After 1924 Odon Lottin went further in his research on the texts of and witnesses to the medieval doctrines of natural law and natural rights. He published a series of articles in the *Ephemerides theologicae Lovanienses* that were later collected in the volume, *Le droit naturel chez saint Thomas d'Aquin et ses prédécesseurs*.[10] He then returned to this topic in his collection, *Psychologie et morale aux XIIe et XIIIe siècles*. According to Lottin, the twelfth- and thirteenth-century debate on *lex naturalis* and *ius naturale* was characterized mainly by two types of matters: first, the nature and content of *lex* and *ius*; and second, its features (i.e., innate, universal, and immutable). The detailed examination of the juridical and theological milieu that Lottin offered was thus the essential premise to a closer historical interpretation of Aquinas's *Summa theologiae*, Ia–IIae, q. 94, where the Dominican master gave his account of natural law.[11]

Through close textual analysis, both Grabmann and Lottin studied the development of concepts and language connected with natural law and natural rights during the age of scholasticism. In their perspective, the medieval debate over natural law and natural rights achieved its most complete doctrinal synthesis with Thomas Aquinas. The doctrine of the Dominican master was the final stage in a long process. Mainly in his *Summa theologiae*, Aquinas offered an account of *lex naturae* and *ius naturae* within the largest framework of the Christian understanding of the notions of *lex*, *natura*, and *ius*. In this sense, Aquinas perfected the definition of one of the cornerstones of what Étienne Gilson called *la philosophie chrétienne*.[12] According to this perspective, the Christian authors, in the twelfth and thirteenth centuries, elaborated an idea of *lex/ius naturae* that resolved the contrast between the ancient philosophical emphasis on the natural foundation of moral discourse and the Christian idea of the crucial role of divine grace. As Aquinas explained in his *Summa*, natural law, that is, the participation of human beings in the eternal law established by God, is nothing else but the natural knowledge of the first principles of practical reason. These principles are submitted to the divine illumination of moral consciousness. Medieval discourse on natural law thus bequeathed to Christian culture a systematic presentation of natural law as part of that hierarchy of laws which from the eternal divine law descended to human positive law.[13] Such a hierarchy, perfectly rational, is also perfectly coherent within the ontological order of creation, because, as Gilson explains, according to medieval authors, natural law is to eternal law as being is to Being (i.e., God).[14]

## The Ground of Political Discourse

Interest in medieval natural law doctrines, and particularly the role of Christianity in the definition of *lex naturae* and *ius naturae*, was not unique to Catholic neo-scholasticism and medievalism. From the last decades of the nineteenth century on, German and British scholars devoted increasing attention to this issue. They debated the content of legal positivism and Bismarck's *Kulturkampf*, looking to the Middle Ages for the origins of the basic elements of modern political and constitutional thought. The debate on the implications of legal positivism was developed particularly in Germany, where it directly involved the interpretation of medieval legal culture. Since Savigny stressed the continuity between Roman law and medieval law and opposed natural law to customary and common law, several scholars have focused on the status of natural law in medieval legal culture. In addition, the effects of legal positivism became interwoven with the political and cultural mood of German *Kulturkampf*, which involved several scholars in a series of studies on medieval canon law.[15]

The German historian Otto von Gierke, from 1868 to 1913, published *Das deutsche Genossenschaftsrecht*, a reaction against the idea that modern political thought is basically characterized by positive law, without any essential foundation in natural law.[16] Part of the third volume of this series (1881), devoted to a study of medieval doctrines on the state and collectivism in Germany, was translated into English by Frederic William Maitland under the title *Political Theories of the Middle Ages* (1900).[17] This English edition was a point of reference for subsequent studies on medieval political doctrines and offered a basic argument for a new evaluation of the role of the church in the construction of the political and legal lexicon later assumed by modernity. Among these ideas were those of *lex naturae* and *ius naturae*, which would be so crucial for the building of modern state theories.[18] Gierke, whose interest was mainly the reconstruction of the origins and historical roots of the German legal system, stressed that the idea of natural law was the answer to the question of the relation between state and law. "How then," wrote Gierke, "was it thinkable that, on the one hand, law ought to exist by, for and under the State, and that, on the other hand, the State ought to exist by, for and under the Law?"[19] Natural law, that is, law that exists before the state and limits and regulates the power of the state, was the answer to such questions, the German scholar noted, given by decretists and legists, along with philosophers and theologians, who made use of the classical and patristic heritage.[20] Gierke's research provided a strong historical argument against the positivist doctrine of sovereignty, insofar as it stressed the existence of a legal and political tradition that grounded the state in a natural law that fixed the limits of its power. Generally speaking, Gierke noted that, according to a medieval intellectual perspective, all human authorities and powers, secular and ecclesiastical, were under the *lex naturae*. He stressed the importance of the formulation of the idea of natural law in the theological system of medieval Christianity: it is here that such a concept assumed its proper features. The modern theorists of natural law doctrines (Grotius, Hobbes, Pufendorf, Althusius) inherited and secularized this Christian idea of natural law.[21]

Robert Warraud Carlyle and Alexander James Carlyle developed Gierke's basic idea that medieval Christianity was the framework within which the concept of natural law was defined.

Especially in the fifth volume of their *History of Mediaeval Political Theory* (1903), the two scholars presented the basic ideas of medieval political thought.[22] Following Gierke, they stressed that natural law was not just part of the ancient Greco-Roman inheritance, but moreover was a proper result of medieval thought. Their position was elaborated on the basis of the debate about the foundation of sovereignty and continued what Maitland started with his English translation of Gierke's book. The *History of Mediaeval Political Theory* stressed that the cornerstone of medieval political debate was the principle of the supremacy of law, since medieval authors had no theory of sovereignty. "Natural law," as it was defined mainly by Gratian and Thomas Aquinas, was the set of moral rules that limits political authority. According to the two English scholars, Aquinas did offer a complete account of the nature of law, showing how "natural law" is connected with that "light of natural reason" by which human beings can distinguish good and evil.[23] This preeminence of law over authority is the foundation of that "Rule of Law" which was crucial in modern political and constitutional tradition, mainly in England.[24]

In his 1907 volume devoted to political theories from Gerson to Grotius, John Neville Figgis developed this line and presented political history between the late Middle Ages and the early modern era as a great and constant struggle between civil and religious powers that led to the definition of the basic elements of modern constitutionalism.[25] Figgis described Aquinas's political theory as "the beginning of the later medieval rationalising political thought."[26] The Dominican master was seen as a conscious user of the heritage of ancient Roman legal tradition, combined with the arguments that came from the Church Fathers and founded on the philosophical content of Aristotle's *Politics*. For Figgis, Aquinas's natural law doctrine represented the means through which modern political thought inherited the medieval idea of limits on authorities and powers. For the English scholar, medieval *ius naturale* entails both individual human beings and the existence of a higher legal order.[27]

Figgis developed Gierke's question about the nature of authority and power and their limits and boundaries. He explained that the *lex naturae* and *ius naturae* of medieval authors were limits to the exercise of absolute political power. They represented the very basis on which in the modern era the constitutional tradition built its idea of the state and was radically put in question by those "men like Machiavelli and Hobbes, whose aim is to remove all restraints to the action of rulers except those of expediency."[28]

## Laws, Natures, and Rights

The writings of Gierke and Figgis, as well as the historical account of Carlyle, represented a reaction against the basic assumption of legal positivism, which denies any value to natural law as the basis of any legal system. The crisis of political and legal systems between the two world wars incited the arguments in favor of a reconsideration of the historical value of natural law. Legal positivism had criticized the value of the idea of natural law, mainly stressing the concept of positive law as obligatory command and dismissing matters concerning the essence of law and of the ideal legal standards as irrelevant to jurisprudence. According to authors such as Kelsen, natural law was a suspect concept, inasmuch as it entails that it is not the state that grounds the legitimacy of the legal order.[29] Furthermore, in his view, the phrase "natural law" itself implies a misuse of the word *nature*, here indicating not the physical order of reality but a universal set of moral principles that rational beings can understand and to which they have to conform. Kelsen stressed that the notion of natural law necessarily involves a religious character and an unclear passage from what "is" in nature to what "ought to be" in legal and moral fields.[30]

Totalitarianism and World War II showed the limits of this kind of criticism of natural law. Legal positivism appeared incapable of any form of resistance to authoritarian exercise of political power. On one side, there was the need for strong limits to regulate political authorities; on the other side, there was the will to order the legal system to respect human rights, now perceived not as established by the state but as natural features of individual human beings.[31]

The two tendencies gave rise to new approaches to the topics of natural law and natural rights.

In 1950 Alessandro Passerin d'Entrèves published his *Natural Law: An Introduction to Legal Philosophy*.[32] The Italian scholar showed the importance of natural law in the construction of the European legal culture, analyzing the plurality of traditions and inheritances that characterized its contemporary understanding. Taking into account the historical and philosophical inquiries of the previous decades on this issue, Passerin d'Entrèves argued for the need to combine consciousness of the evolution that the meaning of *lex naturae* (or *lex naturalis*) had undergone over two millennia with a careful philosophical analysis of the debated aspects of this notion.[33] In this way, he distinguished his approach from both the purely historical and purely philosophical perspectives.

In relation to the history of the idea of natural law, Passerin d'Entrèves identified three main stages. In antiquity Romans understood it as something external and formal, which united all humankind under a single legislative standard, while medieval authors, mainly canonists and theologians, considered natural law the basic and immutable criterion for good moral conduct, that is, an internal and rational point of reference for moral life whose value rests on its grounding in the will of God.[34] Thus medieval authors presented natural law as the supreme parameter for evaluating human laws. The passage to modernity, Passerin d'Entrèves noted, entailed a new and significant shift in the understanding of natural law, since the modern age proposed a completely different idea of "nature" from that of the Middle Ages.[35] After the sixteenth century "nature" was no longer synonymous with "creation" but indicated a force independent from God. Philosophers started to ground the validity of natural law not on divine will but on human reason.[36] According to the Italian scholar, this new idea of natural law was rationalistic and individualistic and was the basis on which modern natural law theorists opposed the "self-evident" rights to absolute governments and political powers.

Alongside this historical account, Passerin d'Entrèves developed a philosophical inquiry that he articulated in three ways. First, he noted, the proper essence of law is defined by its function, which is to qualify rather than to command.[37] Second, he explained that the relation between law and morality appears problematic in the context of legal positivism. On the contrary, natural law doctrine is clearer in defining the complex relations between the two fields. Therefore, the notion of natural law combines a clear distinction between law and morals with the clear consciousness of their mutual relations.[38] Third, thanks to these features, natural law is a useful measure for the evaluation of the validity of human laws.[39]

Passerin d'Entrèves's account of natural law summarizes the intellectual situation at the middle of the twentieth century. Natural law became one of the great issues of scientific research in several fields. Jurists and philosophers, as well as theologians and historians, started to rethink the idea of natural law as the possible ground of legal and moral order. Passerin d'Entrèves, in his study of natural law, tried to overcome the limits of legal positivism, which had dominated European legal culture since the last decades of the nineteenth century. In the age of the Universal Declaration of Human Rights, he explained how the modern concern for human rights as limits to the absolute power of government and as the basic criteria to validate human positive laws is nothing but the evolution of the doctrine of natural law in modern times. According to his perspective, the medieval developments of natural law doctrines were the results of the intellectual work of canonists and theologians.[40] Medieval Christian authors are thus considered responsible for one of the crucial transitions in the history of natural law doctrines and in the definition of some basic questions concerning the grounds of the legal and political order.

## QUESTIONS AND DOUBTS

Several scholars have remarked that the first use of *ius naturale* as the right of individual human beings can be found before the usually accepted beginning of the modern age. Studying the texts of medieval authors, they have shown that a subjective understanding of *ius naturale* is explicitly present before Suárez, Grotius, or Locke. The scientific debate about the evolution of *lex naturalis* and *ius naturale* since the late Middle Ages certainly concerns the identification of a "Copernican moment" in the history of natural rights. At the same time, this debate involves a more basic issue: the distinction between the medieval and modern periods.

This chronological distinction comes into question in a new light if we consider the basic features of Otto Brunner's and Reinhart Koselleck's *Begriffsgeschichte* (history of concepts), according to which the passage from the medieval to the modern world is the only real turning point in history.[41] "Conceptual thinking," which is a charactistic particular to modern epistemology, would mark the beginning of scientific knowledge not only in science but also in the humanities. From this point of view, "natural rights theory" would have been born in 1661, when Samuel Pufendorf became the first professor of *ius naturae et gentium* in Heidelberg. The German jurist's teaching would mark the passage from a doctrinal sequence, begun with Aristotle and Cicero and continued during the Middle Ages, to a conceptualized and unified theory of natural right, a cornerstone of modern political thought.[42]

If a theory of subjective natural rights is a crucial feature of modern Europe, its first elaboration could be considered the starting point of the modern age in relation to political doctrine. In this sense, how must the medieval roots of natural rights be considered? What is the relation between the writings of Hobbes or Locke to those of the late medieval canonists or theologians? Did a break in intellectual history marking the beginning of modernity as the age of natural rights really occur? Or was there continuity between the late Middle Ages and modernity in the use of *ius naturale*? Do we have to look for a radical turning point at all, or should we approach the period between the twelfth and eighteenth centuries as a long intellectual shift in the language to our modern meaning of "natural law" and "natural rights"?

In the following pages I deal with these questions and examine a vast intellectual debate, stressing in the conclusion the need for caution about the issue of "the beginning of modernity" in relation to natural law and natural rights theories. In particular, I show that scientific research highlighted a plurality of elements that deal with the passage from the Middle Ages to modernity. Evaluating and connecting the different approaches and contributions, I suggest how complex and articulated is the role of the concepts of *lex naturalis* and *ius naturale* in marking this historical transition.

*Chapter 1*

# OBJECTIVITY VERSUS SUBJECTIVITY

In the past sixty years historians started from either the premise of objectivity or that of subjectivity to debate the relation between modern theories of human rights and medieval accounts of *ius naturale* and *lex naturalis*. For authors such as Michel Villey, modern theories of human rights have their roots in the crisis of the Christian late medieval philosophical order.[1] Against an idea of human rights that he considered the product of juridical subjectivism and legal positivism, Villey supported a return to the tradition that combines Aristotle, Aquinas, and the Roman jurists.[2] In contrast, scholars such as Brian Tierney assumed that the relation between the Middle Ages and modernity cannot be reduced simply to opposition between the Christian medieval moral and legal orders and the modern system of "subjective rights."[3] Rather, in their view, a more complex and longer process created a deep connection between the modern theories of natural rights and medieval accounts of *lex naturalis* and *ius naturale*.

## THE CONSTRUCTION OF A HARMONIOUS SYSTEM OF NATURAL LAW AND NATURAL RIGHTS

In his first studies devoted to Roman legal tradition, published in 1956, Villey stresses how there is no trace at all of a subjective

13

meaning of *ius* in the entire set of laws and jurisprudence produced in ancient Rome; on the contrary, the term means a fair state of affairs.[4] According to Villey, Roman jurists used the term *ius* in an objective sense, as synonymous with *dominium*, which here does not indicate a right but a state of things preceding law and that law can limit.[5] Even if several passages of the ancient Roman jurisprudence seem to employ *ius* in the sense of "right," Villey always denied such an interpretation. He firmly held that ancient Roman jurists never used *ius* to indicate a right.

This understanding of the ancient Roman notion of *ius* is crucial for Villey's account of the origin of modern natural rights theory. According to the French scholar, in fact, Roman inheritance is one of the main elements in the development of medieval legal tradition. In his studies of the basis and features of juridical thought, Villey noted that medieval authors combined the vestiges of Roman legal tradition with the moral and ethical implications of Christianity. Assuming this understanding of the late Middle Ages, Villey certainly agrees with the main conclusions reached by historical research in the 1930s and 1940s, which stressed the crucial role of Christian theology in the developments of medieval juridical thought.[6] He notes that all serious research on the foundations of medieval legal culture must examine its theological basis. Particularly crucial for Villey is the scholastic thought of the twelfth and thirteenth centuries, which was the fruit of the so-called *philosophie chrétienne*.[7] In this sense Villey's idea of the passage from antiquity to late antiquity and finally to the Middle Ages is parallel to that offered by Étienne Gilson for the history of philosophy.[8]

Villey distinguished two main periods in the history of the philosophy of law.[9] The age of the Fathers marks the starting point for a process of construction of the Christian rights theory. Augustine of Hippo's writings and doctrines are seen as a complete summary of the results reached by the entire patristic tradition. In his *City of God*, he meditated on the crisis and fall of the Roman Empire, offering to medieval authors the ideal of a perfect political community whose legal sources must be found in the Holy Scriptures. As Villey noted, the "juridical élite" of the High Middle

Ages was educated on the basis of this Augustinian tradition, which dominated the cultural panorama until the development of the twelfth-century schools and their teaching method.[10] Gratian in his *Concordantia Discordantium Canonum* systematized the achievements of this long "Augustinian" tradition. Opening his masterpiece with the equivalence between natural law and the contents of the Old and New Testaments, the medieval master plainly followed the tendency "to absorb the earthly city into the celestial one, to create and organize the city of God on earth."[11]

The twelfth century, with the beginnings of the 'scholastic method', marks an evolution in the idea of law. The masters in canon law, that is, the commentators on Gratian's *Decretum*, prepared the field for the rise of a veritable system of law, which was fully elaborated in the context of university culture during the thirteenth century.[12] In particular, twelfth-century authors, both theologians and canonists, shared a common philosophical interest in the notion of *natura*. According to Villey, their doctrines and ideas about this concept were crucial for all subsequent discussions about natural law and natural rights, including Thomas Aquinas's systematic theory of law.[13] The great Dominican master elaborated his doctrine of law as part of his general project to appropriate Aristotelian philosophy from a Christian perspective.[14] In doing so, he opposed the Augustinian idea that nature is corrupted by original sin. In line with Aristotle, he assumed that human nature has not been completely destroyed by original sin and still maintains the signs of the original order established by God. This state of affairs offers two ways to understand the divine plan, or *lex divina*: revelation and natural reason. According to this perspective, Holy Scripture and natural law are no longer identical: they are two different approaches to divine law, each with specific features but in agreement in terms of their content.

Villey stresses that the human capability to grasp the divine *ordo* of the world and to understand humanity's own proper end clearly shows the existence of a *lex naturalis*. This *lex* is the specific expression of the *lex aeterna*. Natural law, in fact, would be nothing more than the part of eternal law established by God that refers properly to human beings as rational creatures. Human beings, in fact, considering the *bonum* to which their own nature is ordered, can know the precepts and prescriptions of natural law.[15] Villey goes on to explain that Aquinas, with his idea of a "natural" understanding of natural law, also established the limits of natural law and the need for a different approach from the point of view of Christian faith. Natural law is in fact connected with human cognitive capabilities and their intrinsic limitations, as well as with changes in the contingencies caused by human freedom.[16] Aquinas based on these elements the need for a positive law, adding a third "Aristotelian" justification: the political and social nature of human being that makes the creation of an institutional order necessary.[17] According to this interpretation of Aquinas, natural law is the common moral basis established with respect to the *bonum* to which human nature is ordained as something rationally created. His discussion of natural law also includes the notion of *ius naturale* as an objective right, that is, a moral precept with a mutable character by reason of the changes in human nature. Thomas, Villey notes, gave to the general moral rule, "do good and avoid evil," a simple formal value, since human beings adapt this general rule to their contingencies.[18] Because of the objective and mutable character of *ius naturale* as a set of moral principles, Aquinas connected precepts and moral rules to the Aristotelian ethics of virtue and to the complex psychological structure of moral action.

According to Villey, Aquinas presents a harmonious theory of natural law and objective natural rights, based on solid metaphysical ground. God himself, because of his goodness and wisdom, creates the political dimension as the proper feature of human being. Villey notes that Aquinas, assuming the Aristotelian doctrine of four causes, traced an image of the world as harmoniously ordered with respect to specific ends and clearly understandable as such by human reason. Aquinas places natural law on this ground, that is, in the range of features of human beings as rational creatures and thus ordered to act freely. More generally, in Villey's view, Aquinas fully reintroduced the content of Aristotelian political science to European culture, fixing some crucial points of reference for the debate on the modern state in the following centuries. In fact, Aquinas's discussion of the idea of "Right" was at the origin of an attempt to adapt the system of law to an evolving European framework whereby secular institutions, such as monarchies and the commons, became the new political actors.[19] Moreover, the Dominican master provided an account of the notion of *lex* that would be crucial for the evolution of modern juridical systems.

## The Inventor of Modern Natural Rights

Villey explains that Thomism is a system of thought with respect to which a break soon occurred. This break was the starting point of a descending parable if not an interruption of the elaboration of a complete Christian juridical culture. It was this break that, according to Villey's chronology of the history of legal philosophy, marked the beginning of a third period, the protagonist of which is the Franciscan theologian William of Ockham.[20] Villey considers Ockham the founder of the modern idea of natural rights as subjective rights. In this he was deeply influenced by Georges de Lagarde, according to whom the English master is the first champion of natural rights and is responsible for the secularization of Law and Right.[21]

The reasons for the novelty of Ockham's ideas and the break with the previous tradition of "Christian philosophy" can be found in the very basis of his philosophical thought. According to de Lagarde and Villey, Ockham's radical nominalism drove theology to bring into question the notion of *ordo naturalis*, in order to affirm the complete freedom of God's will.[22] Duns Scotus had already stressed the need to preserve God's *potentia absoluta* (absolute power) and his consequent freedom from the limitations imposed by a supposed natural order.[23] Ockham would have denied the existence of a natural order and stressed, on the contrary, the real existence of simple individual realities.

Ockham's nominalism marks a crisis in the metaphysical idea of nature and of the connection between language and reality, bringing about radical changes in the notions of Law and Right as well. "Natural law" and "natural rights" are no longer denominations of an objective set of norms and rules, which is at the basis of the juridical science. Dissolving the metaphysical consistency of nature through his nominalism, Ockham removed the possibility of establishing juridical solutions starting with nature. It is the individual human being, that is, the only existing moral reality, who has to be put at the center of juridical science. The main interest of this science is, then, to describe the juridical qualities of this individual, his faculties and his subjective rights.[24] According to this perspective, in Ockham's philosophical system there is no place for natural law, because the only authority on which rules and precepts rest is divine will. Therefore, Villey concludes, nominalism created the premises for juridical positivism, for without any reference to objective natural law, only the individual will justify the existence of prescriptions or precepts. Moreover, Villey finds in Ockham's perspective the loss of the universal character of law, because it is linked only to the legislator's will.[25]

According to Villey, Ockham is the father of modern individual rights, and his doctrine is the basis on which several successors developed their arguments. Authors such as Jean Gerson and Gabriel Biel and, later, Hobbes, Locke, and Bentham would inherit the content of the *Opus nonaginta dierum*, in which the radical change from the previously used language to the modern language of natural rights first appeared. In this work, Villey remarks, Ockham devoted his intellectual energy to the polemics on poverty between Franciscans and Pope John XXII. Discussing notions such as *ius utendi*, *potestas licita*, *usus facti*, and *ius poli*, the Franciscan master used the term *ius* in a more restricted sense—as an individual power of human being, which became the modern definition of *right*.[26] According to Villey, Ockham's philosophy was the crucial turning point, the main development of which he saw as occurring with the seventeenth-century École du droit naturel. The members of this "school," Grotius, Pufendorf, and Thomasius, aimed to create an entire system of "natural subjective rights," which formed the basis of modern juridical achievements like the civil code.

CHRISTIANITY AND MODERNITY
IN LIGHT AND SHADE

Villey's doctrine of the history of the concept of *ius naturale* was the source of a large and long debate. The French scholar's idea that the history of Western European philosophy of law was marked by a radical break caused by Ockham's theory of rights gave rise to further studies as well as critiques and new interpretations. Certainly Villey offered a clear and complete vision of the development of European intellectual history between the late Middle Ages and the early modern era. Considering the twelfth and thirteenth centuries as the age of natural law theory, followed by the beginning of the age of natural rights theory, he assumed some elements of the idea of historical development proper of other French scholars such as de Lagarde and Étienne Gilson. Generally speaking, in fact, all these authors stress that European culture, since the age of Anselm of Canterbury, Ivo of Chartres, Abelard, and Gratian, was characterized by the progressive building of a harmonious system of thought, where the ancient heritage (both philosophical and legal) was combined within a general Christian framework. Medieval authors merged ancient doctrines with the theological heritage of Augustine and the other Fathers of the Church. According to this interpretation, Thomas Aquinas's writings contain a higher and more perfect expression of the harmonious combining of these different traditions. What follows after the composition of William of Ockham's *Opus nonaginta dierum* is the development of a completely different system of thought, namely, the cultural perspective of the modern age.

Villey's account of the history of European culture certainly stressed the crucial role of Christianity in the development of philosophical and legal thought during the Middle Ages. Considering the specific topic of natural law and natural rights, Villey's account remarks on the importance of the theological debate to determine their semantic value. At the same time, in his *Leçons d'histoire de la philosophie du droit* and *La formation de la pensée juridique moderne*, he summarizes a series of doubts and questions.

The idea that the history of natural rights theory was marked by a radical break in the development of a harmonious and "humanistic" synthesis of ancient Roman legal tradition and Christian theology seems to be an ideological assumption rather than the conclusion of a careful historical analysis of sources and texts. Villey notes that the sign of this break is the use of the expression *ius naturale* to define a "subjective right," that is, a power or faculty proper to an individual human being. According to Villey, as discussed above, this use was unknown before Ockham's *Opus nonaginta dierum*. Such an assumption appears to be quite strange, considering the fact that before Villey's studies, during the 1920s and 1930s, Martin Grabmann and Odon Lottin had offered a series of clear references to legal, philosophical, and theological writings dating to between the twelfth and thirteenth centuries, in which *ius naturale* also has a "subjective" value.

Villey does not contemplate a study of the semantic evolution of terminology during the medieval period. Furthermore, this was the logical and coherent consequence of the idea that a subjective value of "natural right" was the main outcome, on a legal and moral plane, of nominalism. This doctrine, based on a metaphysics that gives consistency only to individual entities, understands "natural rights" as features of the individual human being. There is no place for an objective moral rule based on natural order, because, according to Villey's understanding of William of Ockham's doctrine, there is no natural order in nature and thus no natural law but just what divine will has established. It is clear that Villey presents the changing of metaphysical doctrine as the real cause of the break between the age of natural law and the age of natural rights. It is the passage from realism to nominalism that could have produced the emergence of the new theory of subjective rights.

This historical analysis is based on the implicit assumption that the intellectual history of Europe, and in particular the history of philosophy, has to be seen as a sequence of systems that provide a holistic account of reality. In this sense Aquinas and Ockham are the champions, not just of two theories of law and right, but, more generally, of two different philosophical systems. Therefore, the content of a theory of law and right rests on a metaphysical foundation and is coherent with the kind of order of the world that is defined and established.

It is questionable whether this is the case with the history of philosophy in general or the history of the ideas of law and right in particular. Villey considers medieval authors who frequently debated these concepts in different situations, often in reply to certain political or religious contingencies. Ockham, for instance, offered his account of law and rights in the context of his long conflict with the popes rather than in his more systematic theological expositions. Similar considerations could be made about Aquinas and the other crucial authors that dealt with these topics. The existence and nature of a direct and inescapable connection between philosophy of law and metaphysics is something that needs careful historical study, considering case by case the content and context of each text.

Connected to this issue also is the problem of the value of Villey's intellectual portrait of Ockham as the founder of modern natural rights theory. The French scholar presents Ockham's political thought as the first account of subjective rights, of the features proper to each individual human being. In doing so, he demonstrates the distinctiveness of Ockham's doctrines with respect to contemporary early fourteenth-century authors as well as to the previous scholastic systems. However, he does not consider the complex relationship of Ockham's account of *ius naturale* with the explicit and implicit sources that the master used. As de Lagarde himself noted, the Venerabilis Inceptor built his philosophy of law in relation to the philosophical and theological heritage of the ancients and late antiquity, as well as of twelfth- and thirteenth-century legal, philosophical, and theological culture. He clearly knew the positions not only of Aquinas and Scotus but also those of the great canonists and legists. He infuses his writings with these kind of references. This suggests that we should consider the "medieval" character of Ockham's work and question the very nature of the relation between innovations and continuities in his doctrine of natural rights.

*Chapter 2*

# THE FOUNDATION
# OF POLITICAL AND
# MORAL ORDER

Since the 1950s scholars have focused on the features of the philosophy of law in the late Middle Ages, especially the fourteenth and fifteenth centuries in order to verify the existence of a break in the evolution of the notion of *ius naturale* that Villey had insisted on. Francis Oakley, Richard Tuck, and John Finnis have debated Villey's interpretation of the rise of modern natural rights theory from different methodological and scientific points of view. From their studies and analysis come some reconsiderations of the history of ideas in medieval western Europe as well as new perspectives on the evolution of the idea of natural rights.

### THE IMPORTANCE OF AN "AGE":
### OAKLEY AND CONCILIARISM

Francis Oakley dealt with natural law and natural rights starting from the intellectual heritage of John Figgis, summarized in his *Political Thought from Gerson to Grotius, 1414–1625*.[1] Figgis had stressed that the origin of modern constitutionalism, and thus also of modern natural rights theory, has to be sought in the elaboration of a conciliar theory during the fourteenth and fifteenth centuries as a solution to the Great Schism. Oakley, in a study devoted to Figgis's basic conclusions, notes that the great historian had presented the conciliar movement as the highest expression of medieval constitutionalism and as "the watershed between the medieval and the modern world."[2]

Oakley remarks on the role of the conciliar movement and agrees that there was continuity between thirteenth-century canonists and fourteenth-century conciliarists as posed by Brian Tierney in his *Foundations of the Conciliar Theory*.[3] In his 1964 study on the political thought of Pierre d'Ailly, Oakley notes that it could be misleading to consider intellectual European history of the late Middle Ages simply as a dialectic confrontation between realism and nominalism. The novelty and plurality of late medieval political, legal, and philosophical debates cannot be reduced to simple scholastic controversies between the exponents of two philosophical parties. Considering the intellectual biography of authors such as d'Ailly, in fact, the influence not just of a single school or tradition but of all the main philosophical perspectives of the time is evident.[4] Oakley, considering the traditions of ideas, doctrines, and languages that run from the thirteenth through the fifteenth century, focuses his research on a larger and more articulated vision of the relation between different historical periods.

The existence of continuities does not entail the absence of difference and change in the sequence of doctrines and intellectual movements, however. As Villey had already noted, fourteenth-century European culture is deeply marked by the new nominalism championed by William of Ockham.[5] Oakley agrees with the French scholar in considering this new philosophical perspective the main element of novelty and change in the understanding of natural law and natural right as well. Otherwise, he denies that Ockham and his nominalism marked a radical break with the immediately preceding philosophy of law and right. Following Gordon Leff's judgment, he identifies the specific features of fourteenth-century culture with a desire "to disengage faith from reason."[6] This evolution in the relation between faith and reason is the key innovation not just of Ockham, but of an entire generation of intellectuals. The development of this new cultural disposition, more than the writings of a single author, caused the redefinition of the basic notions of *lex*, *ius*, and *natura*.[7]

Nominalism is the philosophical and metaphysical framework within which the conciliar movement grew up. According to Oakley, in fact, the authors involved in the long and complex "constitutional" debate about the nature of the church dealt with the definition of "natural law" and "natural right" and elaborated an idea of subjective rights whose features seem close to the modern notion of human natural rights. What the English scholar offers in his research is thus not the image of a break in intellectual history but the idea that at the origin of modern natural rights theory there is a process with a crucial transition in the decades from the fourteenth to the fifteenth century. This "Age of Conciliarism" is a forge where ancient ideas and earlier doctrinal traditions were reworked and new meanings were given to expressions such as *ius naturale*.

Oakley develops a different and alternative explanation of the evolution in the history of the origin of modern natural law and natural rights theories with respect to Villey. Nevertheless, he shares with Villey a crucial consideration: the idea of the existence of an inescapable link between metaphysics and natural rights theory. According to Oakley, nominalism, with its individualistic turn, was the basis of the elaboration of conciliarists. The new philosophical perspective, fearing a necessitarianism that could limit God's freedom and will, focused on the individual human being.[8] This care for preserving God's omnipotence, in Oakley's opinion, was the consequence of a theological concern first expressed in Étienne Tampier's 1277 condemnation of several propositions, including some Thomistic assertions. For Oakley, the 1277 condemnation and fourteenth-century nominalism shared a basic intention: to stress the radical difference between philosophy and theology, that is, to claim the specific features of theology and its complete independence from philosophical influences.[9]

Ockham's philosophical account has to be placed in the cultural framework that started with the 1277 condemnation. Ockham's radical distinction between absolute and ordained divine power,

Oakley affirms, shared the concern of Tampier's decree and links the doctrine of natural rights of the Franciscan master with previous debate. In this sense Oakley rejects Villey's opinion that the author of the *Opus nonaginta dierum* had canceled the notion of "natural law" in favor of a simple "divine positive law." Ockham, on the contrary, proposed a theory of natural law as something posed by God's divine will, as the "absolute, immutable, and admitting of no dispensation" law that belongs to "the framework of ordained and ordinary power of God."[10] Ockham appears to be the clearest theorist of the so-called legal voluntarism with which the majority of the conciliarists agree. Gerson, d'Ailly, Gabriel Biel, Jacques Almain, John Mair, and Alphonse de Castro proposed a voluntarist theory of natural law. The protagonists of the age of reform, both Catholic and Protestant, such as Martin Luther, John Calvin, and Francisco Suárez, also seem to be well acquainted with this perspective. A chain, according to Oakley, goes forward from fourteenth-century nominalism to the *ius naturale* of Grotius and Pufendorf, as well as to the legal and political thought of Hobbes and Locke.[11]

This perspective suggests that Ockham can be seen as the author of a reform of the semantic value of the crucial terms *lex naturae* and *ius naturae* rather than the father of modern rights theory. In his political writings he debated and criticized Aquinas's theory of natural law starting from the different metaphysical premises of nominalism in order to ground natural law on a voluntarist basis, that is, on the dispositions of the divine will. As Oakley explains, the Franciscan theologian shows a new reading of the Pauline dictum "omnis potestas a Deo" (Rom. 13:1). Natural law still remains a point of reference for moral life and also for political discourse.[12] Conciliarists, mainly the Parisians, supported the idea that the foundation of legitimate public authorities, both civil and ecclesiastical, rests on natural law.[13] They use the term *lex naturae* to refer to law created by God to rule animate and inanimate beings, rational and nonrational creatures. This law is relevant to the juridical field. Oakley notes that for authors like Pierre d'Ailly, natural law consists of the series of obligations and prescriptions established by divine will and immediately evident to human reason.[14]

Divine will is the proper authority to establish natural law; similarly, a "properly constituted law-making authority" is the only basis for legitimate positive law in the field of political theory.[15] In this sense, the relation between God and natural law based on God's divine will is the basic model for every legitimate legislative authority. Oakley, in fact, notes that, according to a voluntarist perspective, the legislator (i.e., the proper authority) establishes positive law. Therefore, he suggests, nominalism, the distinction between absolute and ordained divine power, individualism, and voluntarism have been features of the philosophical, theological, and legal cultures since the beginning of the fourteenth century and that Ockham shared them with other contemporaries and followers. According to Oakley, all the conciliarists, from d'Ailly to Jean Gerson, from Francesco Zabarella to John of Ragusa or Nicolas Tudeschis, belonged to this intellectual background.[16] Oakley stresses the common basis and interests of these authors but also their differences precisely with respect to the notions of *ius naturale* and *lex naturalis*. In their writings, the account of individual moral life of individual human beings is part of a discourse that aims to define and establish legitimate authority. What they offered to their followers was a redefinition of the key terms of moral and political discourse: right, morality, will, practical reason, authority, and power. In doing so, Oakley notes, their intellectual engagement represented not a break but a link between the age of medieval scholasticism and modern political thought.[17]

## Ius as Dominium: The Stages of the Medieval Evolution according to Richard Tuck

Both Villey and Oakley, even if for different reasons, stress the importance of the fourteenth-century philosophical, theological, and legal debates with respect to the rise of modern natural rights theory. Such an idea of the historical development of the notions of natural law and natural rights influenced scholars like Isaiah Berlin and Michel Bastit.[18] But since the 1970s studies devoted to these issues have focused more accurately on textual analysis of the meaning of the key expressions *ius naturae* (or *naturale*) and *lex naturae* (or *naturalis*) in the late Middle Ages.

Richard Tuck offers the first significant example of the fruitfulness of this method. In his *Natural Rights Theories*, he moves from a quotation of the *Summa summarum* of the Dominican theologian Silvestro Mazzolini da Prierio (1506), according to which there are two different meanings of the Latin term *ius*.[19] On the one side, it means "something the operation of which its possessor could control himself"; that is, *ius* is synonymous with *dominium* and indicates a possession, a property. On the other side, the term refers to something that is not under the control of the man who possesses it but depends on the recognition of other people. This is what Mazzolini called *iura*, "rights."[20]

Tuck quotes the fifteenth-century Italian theologian in order to underline that in that period there was clearly a distinction between an "active" and a "passive" sense of *ius*. In fact, when Mazzoleni speaks of *ius* as a faculty, the action of which is under the control of the agent, he is clearly using the Latin term in an active sense. On the contrary, when he uses *iura* to indicate something that depends on the recognition of others, he adopts a passive sense. According to Tuck, Mazzoleni made a "paradigmatic" distinction, which summarized the crucial features of the language of rights at the beginning of the sixteenth century. Mazzoleni's definition of what a "right" is appears to be quite close to what will be found in the great seventeenth-century debates about rights.[21]

Starting from this consideration of the early sixteenth-century situation, Tuck goes back to find out the origin of this use of *ius* as *dominium* in an active sense, which marks the beginning of modern natural rights. In relation to Villey's studies on modern natural rights theory, he first criticizes the analysis of the heritage of the ancient Roman jurists that Villey offered in his writings. As noted above, Villey assumed that both Roman jurists and early glossators did not have any concept of subjective right. This meaning of the term *ius* would be elaborated only by William of Ockham in his *Opus nonaginta dierum* in the first half of the fourteenth century.

According to the French scholar, the Romans used the term *ius* not in the sense of *dominium*, that is, "property," but to define an objective state of things. Tuck notes that if it is true that Romans used *ius* differently with respect to us, this does not imply that they had no "subjective" understanding of it. In the writings of Roman jurists there is certainly an objective use of *ius*, according to which this term means an objective and discoverable rule, that is, a "law." However, the authors of the ancient Roman legal tradition also adopted a "subjective" use of *ius* to indicate the right relation between two disputants, that is, the correct and just bilateral relationship between two individuals and neighbors that creates an *obligatio*.[22] Paulus, Gaius, and the other Roman jurists used *ius* in this way.

On this basis, Tuck rejects Villey's interpretation and traces a different account of the origin of modern natural rights theory. The "subjective" idea of right was, in fact, a heritage of the ancient Roman tradition rediscovered by the early glossators and legists at the end of the eleventh century and the beginning of the twelfth. For Tuck, the Bolognese glossators, from Irnerius on, were the first who elaborated the concept of *ius* as "right," starting from the Roman idea that *ius* could mean something that two men mutually recognize to each other. Irnerius, Tuck notes, affirmed the idea of the equivalence between *dominium* and *ius*, stressing the fact that *dominium* is a kind of *ius*, and the early glossators developed the idea of "passive" rights, something that receives the recognition of others. This peculiar perspective, Tuck notes, was due to the needs to which the glossators responded: to meld the legal language of the early Middle Ages, influenced by the culture of Germanic kingdoms, with the Roman legal heritage rediscovered through the *Digest*.[23]

Azo, at the end of the twelfth and the beginning of the thirteenth century, offered the first synthesis of this new legal culture in his writings. This Bolognese master introduced the distinction between (1) *iura in re* and (2) *iura pro re* (or *ad rem*). According to Tuck, (2) indicates a claim on something that a man does not yet possess, while (1) indicates properly a *dominium*, that is, something that is actually in the possession of man. This distinction corresponds to that between the concepts *ususfructum* (usufruct) and *dominium* (property).[24] The glossators developed their discourse, always considering only passive rights, so that rights would be claims that "required other men to act in some way to the claimant, to grant him something." Tuck then notes that while civil lawyers developed a theory of "passive" rights, the contemporary canonists elaborated an "active" idea of rights as powers.[25]

It is at this stage that a second turning point in the evolution of the natural rights discourse occurred. Tuck identifies this turning point with the contents of Accursius's *Gloss* to the *Corpus iuris civilis*. If twelfth-century glossators distinguished between "property" (*dominium*) and "usufruct," Accursius introduced the concept of *dominium utile* to indicate what the usufructuary possesses. This *dominium* is distinct from the *dominium directum*, which is proper to the higher lord. Tuck stresses the fact that the phrase *dominium utile* indicates any *ius in re*, that is, a property right that could be defended against all other men.[26] Every kind of right has been seen as referring to the individual's own property. It is precisely this meaning of *ius* as property that, in Tuck's view, will extend its influence to the seventeenth-century theorists of natural rights.[27] The successors and followers of Accursius, for example, Jacques de Révigny, Pierre Belleperche, and Bartolus de Sassoferrato, developed the concept of *dominium utile*. This idea can be found also in other contemporary medieval theorists of natural rights, such as Thomas Aquinas.[28] Tuck notes, in fact, that the Dominican master did have knowledge of the Accursian concept of *dominium utile*, thanks to which he could understand the basic concept of right commonly used by glossators. The scholar quotes *Summa theologiae* Ia–IIae, q. 94, a. 5, to prove that Aquinas had an idea of right taken from contemporary glossators, even if he did not think that men have at first sight a right to natural liberty.[29]

A third turning point occurred in the fourteenth century. In Tuck's view, this was a long period of change and debate about natural rights theory, starting from the diffusion of the writings and ideas of Duns Scotus. The Franciscan master, in fact, would be the first who, bringing into question Aquinas's system, started a radical reconsideration of the notions of *dominium* and *ius* within the framework of the controversy about "apostolic poverty." Furthermore, Duns Scotus considered *ius naturale* not neutral with respect to the notion of property (*dominium*).[30] He remarks that if the adjective *naturale* reminds us of the original state of nature proper of human beings before the fall, *ius* indicates the *communis usus* (common use), which is the proper relation between human beings and things in the state of innocence. In this case *ius naturale* has a positive value and indicates just the *usus facti* as properly natural, while *dominium*, that is, individual property, does not belong to the original state of nature.[31] Tuck considers the development of this doctrine among the Franciscans as the main reason for the rise of the controversy about "poverty" between the order of Saint Francis and the papal curia of John XXII in Avignon. According to the pope's bull *Quia vir reprobus*, God's *dominium* over earth is the model of man's *dominium* over his possessions. In this sense, Tuck notes, *dominium* is a "natural right" because it is a feature of the human state of nature, and all the relations between man and his goods are examples of *dominium*.[32]

William of Ockham reacts against this account of "natural right," and thus his ideas concerning the *ius naturale* have to be considered within the great debate about Franciscan poverty. Whereas Villey remarked on the absolute novelty of Ockham's ideas and lexicon and saw him as the real father of modern natural rights theory, Tuck assumes the entire controversy over poverty is crucial to the framework for understanding the position of the English theologian.[33] This event, in fact, should be seen as a sort of anticipation of the definition of *dominium* as proper to the state of nature, which will be crucial in the seventeenth-century debate about individual property. According to Tuck, Ockham's works and doctrines have to be evaluated in light of the historical and doctrinal turning point of the debate about poverty. In this sense they influenced successive authors like Jean Gerson, who was engaged in the redefinition of the notions of *ius* and *facultas*.[34]

Tuck's analysis of the development of natural rights theory, therefore, presents the controversy over apostolic poverty as the crucial battlefield from which emerged the modern concept of rights. The discussion about the notion of *dominium* creates the premises for the seventeenth-century elaboration of the idea of individual property, particularly because *dominium* started to be seen as the relation between a man and his goods, analogous to the relation between God and the world. These ideas constitute the basis on which Jean Gerson built a theory of natural rights, which would dominate the European legal and political culture until the last decades of the sixteenth century. According to Tuck, Gerson was the first scholar who gave an explicit definition of *ius* as a *facultas*, that is, as a power or an "ability" of an individual. In doing this, the theologian assimilated *ius* to *libertas*.[35] Here, Gerson is considered the author of a natural rights theory that assumes *ius* as a power proper to an individual. "Liberty" is this kind of power, while law is a "practical right reason," that is, a rule that directs actions and movements toward their own end. This doctrine, developed and systematized by fifteenth- and sixteenth-century authors like Conrad Summenhart and John Mair, became the common account of natural rights.[36] In Gerson's doctrine Tuck sees the first establishment of the crucial modern distinction between "right" and "law" that is common to all seventeenth-century natural rights theorists.

## From a "Discourse about Doctrines of Natural Law" to a "Discourse about Natural Law"

Shortly after the publication of Richard Tuck's study on the origin of natural law, John Finnis published his volume *Natural Law and Natural Rights*.[37] Finnis's analysis of the two concepts mentioned in his title is properly philosophical rather than historical, but its implications for the debate about the origin of the modern ideas of natural law and natural rights appear to be crucial. The role of Finnis's ideas clearly emerges in relation to the polemical exchange that he has with Tierney over the interpretation of Aquinas's doctrine of *ius naturale*.[38] According to Finnis, the Dominican master also used the phrase *ius naturale* in his writings in a subjective sense; from Tierney's point of view, Aquinas had no natural rights doctrine. However, Tierney notes that Finnis points out an error in Villey's account of Aquinas's position on natural rights. Villey had stressed the radical incompatibility between the doctrinal system of Aquinas and a theory of natural rights as subjective rights. Finnis's study of Aquinas's moral and legal philosophy has shown the philosophical inconsistency of this judgment, but this, Tierney notes, does not mean that Aquinas did have a natural rights theory or at least a use of *ius naturale* in the sense of "natural right."[39]

Finnis replies to Tierney's objections by showing that they disagree on the interpretation of specific passages of Aquinas's *Summa theologiae*, namely, IIa–IIae q. 57, q. 58, and q. 122.[40] As I discuss below, Finnis sees these passages precisely as the basis for the development of a theory of natural rights as part of a more general moral and legal discourse concerning *ius naturale* and *lex naturalis*. The debate with Tierney, even if related to the general understanding of Aquinas's position on natural rights, also concerns the origin of modern natural rights theory. According to Finnis, in fact, if Aquinas really had understood and used *ius naturale* as "natural right," the consequence could be that his philosophical and theological system would represent the foundation of a tradition that leads to modern natural rights theory and to the contemporary concept of human rights.

There are necessary premises to the examination of Finnis's position: first, he assumes a philosophical rather than a historical perspective; and second, his interest in Aquinas and medieval doctrines of *ius naturale* and *lex naturalis* is due to his aim to elaborate a coherent moral and legal system based on natural law and natural rights. In the first pages of *Natural Law and Natural Rights* he clearly distinguishes between "discourse about natural law" and "discourse about a doctrine or doctrines of natural law."[41] He thus sharply distinguishes philosophical inquiry on these issues from the historical study of the different theories and doctrines. In choosing this kind of philosophical approach, Finnis places himself in the methodological line defined by Germain Grisez, who has devoted several studies to Aquinas's doctrine of natural law since 1965. The basic idea of this approach is to develop a philosophical analysis of Aquinas's texts and evaluate their contents according to the coherence and strength of the arguments and reasoning.[42]

Despite these general epistemological premises, Finnis refers several times to the historical antecedents of natural law and natural rights, as when he, for instance, explains that Samuel Clarke's ideas on natural law in the early eighteenth century is preceded by the sixteenth-century doctrines of authors like Grotius, Suárez, and Vazquez.[43] Moreover, Finnis elaborates his account of natural law and natural rights by looking at Aquinas as the most significant author of a synthesis on these topics. In a brief account of the evolution of the modern idea of natural rights, he places Aquinas's doctrine as the better and more complete exposition of the idea of natural rights whose roots are in the ancient Roman legal tradition. In *Summa theologiae* IIa–IIae q. 57, a.1c, ad 1 and ad 2, the Dominican master offers a distinction between four different meanings of *ius*: (1) "the just thing itself," that is, "the fair" or "aright"; (2) "the art by which one knows or determines what is just"; (3) "the place in which what is just is awarded"; and finally (4) "the award of the judge."[44] Finnis then notes that both Suárez and Grotius, at the end of the sixteenth century, gave a different account of *ius*, focusing on a specific meaning, not listed by Aquinas, namely, *ius* as *facultas*, that is, as a kind of moral power proper to every human being. Grotius develops this meaning of *ius* as a power, stressing that in this sense "liberty" is also an *ius* insofar as it is a power that someone has over something. Hobbes, Locke, and Pufendorf and all the seventeenth-century theorists of natural law, Finnis remarks, would have focused on this specific definition of *ius naturale* as "liberty."[45]

Finnis examines the differences between modern natural rights theory and Aquinas's perspective in order to stress how the latter could be the basis for a new philosophical analysis of natural law and natural rights. What in fact emerges from the pages of *Natural Law and Natural Rights* is a picture of Aquinas's account as more complete and systematic than that of modern authors. According to Finnis, the Dominican master was interested in a more careful analysis of the entire semantic range of the lexicon concerning "natural law" and "natural rights" in order to build a comprehensive moral, legal, and political system of thought.[46]

This image of Aquinas and his "excellence" with respect to the panorama of the development of the ideas of *lex naturalis* and *ius naturale* emerges from Finnis's 1998 study.[47] The volume aims to stress the crucial importance of the philosophical analysis of the Dominican master for any discourse about human society and takes the *Summa theologiae* as the most systematic exposition of his thoughts.

Finnis stresses that Aquinas, in his account of *ius*, clearly makes use of two meanings of the term. On the one hand, it indicates what is proper of a man, *quod suum est*, "what is man's right" (*ius suum*). What a man's right is, is what, for a matter of equality, he is entitled to (*quod ei secundum proportionis aequalitatem debetur*).[48] According to Finnis, this sense of *ius* is equivalent to the modern term "right," placing Aquinas at the origin of a theory of natural rights. Aquinas's second sense of *ius* is "norm" or "rule," which is the general term of comparison for practical reason; in this sense, *ius* is a synonym of *lex*.[49]

The two meanings of *ius*, right and law, are deeply connected. Finnis explains that an action according to practical reasonableness requires being guided and shaped by general principles and norms, by the principles of natural reason, namely, *lex naturalis* or *ius naturale*.[50] What Finnis offers, in the end, is the idea that among the natural rights theorists, Aquinas is the first to successfully compose the distinction between natural rights and natural law in a coherent philosophical system. The Dominican master elaborated a doctrine that is still valid for contemporary debate on natural law and natural rights. The validity of this doctrine rests not on a complete historical analysis of its features and contents but on its philosophical coherence and strength, which make it compatible with contemporary philosophical debate.[51]

## Chapter 3

# THE LONG ROAD TO A COMMON LEXICON

Since 2000 a number of scholars have addressed the topics of natural law and natural rights by examining the role of John Locke's doctrines in the development of modern rights theory. One of the main debated points concerns the relations between Locke's account of natural rights and its sources. The controversy is part of a more general debate about the origin of modern natural rights theory: Is Locke the father of what later became the doctrine of human rights? Or is he just the last heir of a tradition that goes back to the late Middle Ages that he reelaborated with respect to his own time? These questions mainly constitute the basis for Brian Tierney's recent studies of Locke, studies that have provoked various reactions.[1]

Tierney, better known as a scholar of medieval canon law, writes that the crucial ideas of the seventeenth-century English political thinker had been present in European political culture since the twelfth century and that the key concepts of his political philosophy—individual consent to government, self-ownership, self-mastery, natural law, and natural rights—are not exclusive to him. According to Tierney, "the content of Locke's work was shaped by the special circumstances of England in the 1680s."[2] However, this does not mean that the author of the *Two Treatises of Government* created a new legal, moral, and political language. Tierney stresses that Locke used "a cluster of ideas" that were part of the common culture of his time and that the main points debated by Locke had been under consideration by legal and moral theorists for generations.[3]

In order to deal with the question of the origin of modern natural law and natural rights theory, Tierney suggests, it is not sufficient to focus only on the identification of the crucial turning points in the history of ideas: it is not sufficient to fix definitions of "natural law" and "natural rights" and to look for their first occurrence. More properly, a historian needs to consider the evolution of these terms through the centuries. Seventeenth-century authors modeled their lexicon on the writings of the great scholastic masters such as Vitoria and Suárez, as well as on the ideas of the first great natural rights theorist, Grotius. Through these means, Tierney notes, Locke and his contemporaries received ideas and doctrines that were already present, for instance, in Gratian's *Decretum*.[4]

Because of this realization, the American scholar assumes a specific chronological range of enquiry and a peculiar historical method of analysis. The definitions of "natural law" and "natural rights" that we find in the writings of Locke and Hobbes and of the seventeenth-century authors are more or less the same as would be sanctioned later in the great American and French declarations of the last decades of the eighteenth century. If these notions have their roots in a culture formed all along the centuries, historical study needs to consider the entire process of their evolution. This process, Tierney suggests, started in the mid-twelfth century, with Gratian's work and with the writings of contemporary and successive canonists. To consider the content of this *longue durée* from 1150 to 1650, Tierney develops a careful textual analysis of many medieval, early modern, and modern writings that dealt with *ius naturale* and *lex naturalis*, highlighting the peculiar features that natural law and natural rights language had in different historical and cultural contexts. This method allows Tierney to delineate the shifts that the key concepts underwent during the five centuries that he considers. Thus the parallels that he traces in medieval ideas and modern doctrines rest on the existence of one common tradition of natural law and natural rights discourse.[5]

## The Roots of a Lexicon

Tierney clearly explains the features of his historical interpretation in his most recent essays: he summarises the basic results of the studies that he has made over several decades in two volumes, *Rights, Laws and Infallibility in Medieval Thought* and *The Idea of Natural Rights*, both published in 1997. These books consist in new editions of Tierney's essays on the history of natural law and natural rights and aim to offer a reconstruction of the development of these ideas.[6]

Tierney's general historical perspective is first defined by a critical analysis of the accounts of Michel Villey and Richard Tuck. Since 1983, in fact, he has submitted the research of the two scholars to careful examination, pointing out their limits and incompleteness.[7] On the one hand, Tierney notes that Villey's view that William of Ockham is the founder of modern rights theory does not consider the importance of the legal, moral, and political sources that Ockham had at his disposal. When Ockham used terms like *ius* or *lex* he had in mind a series of meanings that went back to the juridical culture elaborated since the mid-twelfth century.[8] Moreover, Georges de Lagarde, one of Villey's points of reference, had already stressed the importance of decretists and canonists as sources of the political discourse of the Venerabilis Inceptor. On the other hand, Tierney criticizes Tuck's presentation of the development of the doctrine of subjective rights for focusing on the glossators and their idea of "passive right" and for not considering the importance of the use of *ius* in the work of the canonists.[9] Thus Tierney shows that neither Villey nor Tuck takes into account the importance of the more complex cultural panorama. When Tuck affirms that Gerson is the first author to use *ius* in the sense of *libertas*, for instance, he ignores the fact that Gratian in his *Decretum* wrote about liberties using the phrase *iura libertatis*. In the same way, Villey's idea that Ockham is the founder of modern rights theory because he first used *ius* in terms of *potestas* does not consider that this meaning of *ius* was common among twelfth-century canonists.[10]

Tierney stresses the need for a careful lexical study of the terms "natural law" and "natural rights" in medieval authors. The starting point should be a clear reconstruction of the cultural framework of these authors.[11] Both Ockham and Gerson were well acquainted with legal, moral, and theological notions of late medieval Latin culture. Tierney notes that when Ockham and Gerson understood *ius* as "subjective right" they could refer to several precedents in twelfth-century canon law.[12] According to this perspective the history of the formation of a language of natural law and natural rights started with Gratian's distinction between "natural law" (*ius naturale*) and "customs" (*mores*) with which he opens the *Concordia discordantium canonum*. Gratian, in fact, places *ius naturale* at the basis of his entire juridical structure.[13] The notion of *ius naturale* was the subject of rich analysis by all the following decretists, from Rufinus to Huguccio of Pisa. It is precisely in the writings of these authors that Tierney finds a plurality of meanings according to which *ius naturale* could indicate (1) a force pervading the entire cosmos (according to the Stoic philosophical tradition), (2) a code of moral rules and laws revealed through scripture and accessible to reason, or (3) "a certain force proper of every human creature by nature to do good and avoid the opposite."[14]

The latter meaning of *ius* became common among decretists and canonists. It was used synonymously with the theological term *synderesis*, which indicated precisely the power of the human soul to do good and avoid evil.[15] Moreover, Tierney stresses, the canonists elaborated an early modern rights theory dealing with a series of specific juridical problems. Quite interesting is the example of Huguccio's doctrine according to which a poor man has a "rightful claim" when accused of theft. According to the decretist, such a man could claim this kind of right, even if there was no judicial procedure able to grant things like dignities, dispensations, and alms. The development of the issue by the canonists leads to the elaboration of a sort of judicial protection for the right of the poor man, insofar as the ordinary glosses to the *Decretum* established the bishop's authority to compel an intransigent rich man to give alms to poor people, even if necessary by excommunication.[16] Thus the canonists, Tierney concludes, provided a natural rights theory and created a lexicon and a set of ideas that became part of the common legal and moral culture from the early thirteenth century. Tierney considers the period from 1150 to 1250 as a sort of linguistic and conceptual laboratory where natural rights language was created. Subsequent natural rights theorists built on this heritage in developing their own legal and philosophical culture.

The canonists elaborated a language that also included use of the term *ius naturale* to refer to subjective rights in the sense of "inalienable rights," and this meaning was used by medieval thinkers long before modern debates about natural rights.[17] Tierney offers an example in his analysis of a *quaestio* of the Parisian theologian Henry of Ghent, which dates to 1289.[18] In this study, Tierney stresses the fact that Henry used a specific notion of *ius naturale* that he took precisely from the canonists, and in doing so, he took up a concept of "subjective" natural rights that was absent, for instance, in Aquinas's writings. According to Tierney, the Dominican master cannot be considered the author of a system that coherently combines "objective" natural law and "subjective" natural rights, as Finnis maintains. Rather, Tierney sees Thomas Aquinas as the main representative of an Aristotelian tradition of thought about natural law that has specific features different from the long cultural chain that from Gratian and the decretists goes to Henry of Ghent, Peter John Olivi, Gerson, Summenhart, Vitoria, Suárez, and Grotius.[19]

## A POLITICAL AND LEGAL MATTER: OCKHAM AND GERSON

Tierney supports the idea of a long and continuous tradition of thought of *ius naturale* in "subjective" terms, which crossed the centuries and led to modern natural rights language. William of

Ockham, as well as Jean Gerson and the Dominican masters of the second scholasticism, Grotius, Hobbes, and Locke, contributed to the different stages of this process, adapting to different historical circumstances and needs.

Thus Tierney supports a continuity thesis according to which the writings and movements that other scholars consider crucial turning points in the history of modern natural rights theory are actually passages and stages in a long process. This view, Tierney clarifies, does not entail simply a transmission of ideas and doctrines, where the early fourteenth-century Franciscans, Ockham, Gerson, Summenhart, and Suárez, assumed a passive role. Each of these authors created an original and singular doctrine of natural law and natural rights. They all share the same conceptual tradition and the same legal and moral language that they elaborated and adapted to their own historical context.[20]

In this sense, Ockham's quarrel with the papal curia represents, for Tierney, one of the crucial stages in the development of a subjective notion of *ius naturale*. The Franciscan master, in fact, organized his arguments and replies to the papal pretensions by appealing precisely to the tradition of canon law rather than to his nominalism.[21] Tierney agrees with Oakley in evaluating Ockham's account on natural law and natural rights against the background of the great controversy about apostolic poverty and proceeds to a careful textual analysis of Ockham's writings.[22] In this way he is able to demonstrate the strong influence of the ordinary glosses to the *Decretum* and the *Decretals* on Ockham's political and legal thought. Moreover, Tierney denies one of the crucial elements common to the majority of the previous interpreters of the Venerabilis Inceptor, namely, that his political doctrines rest on his nominalism. According to Villey but also to Oakley and Tuck, the individualism that is at the core of Ockham's nominalism exalts human will as the center of moral life and the origin of moral as well as legal prescriptions. Moreover, the basic distinction between absolute and ordained divine power represents the metaphysical foundation of a new perspective with respect to the previous realism of the Aristotelian and Thomistic perspectives. Tierney stresses the existence of a crucial turn in Ockham's literary production that coincides with the beginning of his conflict with John XXII and his escape from Avignon in 1324.[23] While before this date the master's interests were devoted to philosophical and theological issues, later he was mainly concerned with political disputes. This shift was connected to a turn to different sources and cultural traditions—from philosophical and theological writings to those of canonists and political thinkers. According to this perspective, nominalism, as well as the distinction between absolute and ordained power and voluntarism, was "simply irrelevant to the arguments" that Ockham set out in his political writings.[24]

According to Tierney's historical reconstruction, William of Ockham developed his political perspective from the language and notions of the culture of the canonists and in doing so became part of the long tradition of natural rights as subjective rights. Ockham is thus one of the most important witnesses to this subjective understanding of the notion of *ius naturale*, and this makes him one of the main sources for the great natural rights theorists who followed, especially Gerson.

Deeply engaged in the debates and disputes of the age of the Great Schism, Gerson is seen by Tierney as heir to Ockham's discourse, as well as to previous accounts of natural law and natural rights since the twelfth-century canonists.[25] His literary production can be considered the most complete explanation of the ideas and doctrines of a generation of churchmen, theologians, and canonists who were promoting ecclesiastical reform. Adapting the key concepts and ideas to the historical problems that involved the church at the end of the fourteenth century and the beginning of the fifteenth, Gerson provided a theory of natural rights that included a natural right to liberty, a natural right to self-defense, and a natural right to the necessities of life. Tierney notes that the success of Gerson's writings and ideas among his successors contributes to perpetuating these ideas about *ius naturale*. The main features of Gerson's theory, in fact, can also be found in Almain, Soto, Vitoria, and Suárez as a background for early modern thought on natural rights.[26]

That Gerson, in a certain sense, exemplified the ideas and intellectual perspective of his contemporaries, Tierney stresses, suggests the need for a reconsideration of the importance of conciliarism in the history of the origin of modern natural rights theory. Even if he does not follow Oakley in considering the conciliar theories pervasive and crucial for the rise of a modern rights theory, Tierney remarks on the importance of this intellectual and political movement with respect to the stages of the long process of construction of the modern notion of natural rights.[27] Gerson and the other conciliarists, according to Tierney, were able to rethink the notion of *ius naturale* thanks to their legal and canonistic culture, as well as to their intimate acquaintance with Ockham's theories. This explains how the perspective of conciliarism cannot be evaluated in terms of holistic or individual consideration of natural rights. Such a distinction, which reflects mainly our contemporary understanding of the relation between the general field of natural law and the individual dimension of natural rights, was not proper to Gerson and his contemporaries. On the contrary, according to Tierney, Gerson aimed at reform of the whole church, believing at the same time that there are some intelligible individual rights.[28] Considering subsequent developments in natural rights theory, Tierney evidences the way in which the key concepts and ideas pass from one author to another, so that we find sixteenth-century Dominicans, like Vitoria, engaged in the dispute about the rights of indigenous peoples of the Americas, using *ius naturale* in a sense that was already present in late medieval canonists. The same can be said about the content of Grotius's writings, as well as Locke's theory of individual liberty and natural rights.[29]

From Tierney's perspective, the history of modern ideas of natural law and mainly of natural rights cannot be reduced to the search for a radical turning point or a crucial passage that marks the beginning of a new use of the phrase *ius naturale* as subjective natural right. The continuities and connections between medieval and modern authors, Tierney notes, suggest that this history has to be considered as a long and articulated cultural process whose beginnings go back to the religious culture of the twelfth-century canonists that supplemented rational argumentation about human nature. The shifting "natural rights language" that was shaped between 1150 and 1250, according to Tierney's account, traces the conceptual boundaries of the history of natural rights, since all the following theorists used the lexicon and concepts that early canonists had investigated. Rethinking the meaning and the value of this common cluster of notions, the thinkers who dealt with natural rights from the thirteenth to the seventeenth century elaborated several theories and doctrines and systematic accounts on this issue.

*Chapter 4*

# BREAKS,
# CONTINUITIES,
# AND SHIFTS

Tierney's historical interpretation of the origin of natural rights has given rise to a series of critiques and debates since the 1990s. His *Idea of Natural Rights* especially provoked various reactions: from the harsh and polemical review by Cary Nederman to Charles Reid's careful and accurate presentation of the novelty of Tierney's work.[1] Scholars have debated Tierney's proposition that natural rights theory originated in the work of the twelfth-century canonists and that most of the development of the idea of *ius naturale* occurred between 1150 and 1650. The debate concerning the various meanings of *ius naturale* and *lex naturalis* during the Middle Ages that developed since the end of World War II can be considered part of the long historical discussion about the origin of modern ideas of natural law and natural rights. The past two decades in particular are characterized by a series of methodological and epistemological interventions in the history of natural rights. Some contemporary scholars still consider valid and useful the interpretations of Villey, Tuck, Finnis, and Oakley, while others criticize these different accounts, stressing their limits and problematic aspects.

## "MEDIEVAL" AND "MODERN"
### POLITICAL MENTALITIES

Nederman strikingly criticizes Oakley's view that fourteenth-century conciliarism was the root of modern constitutionalism and thus of modern natural rights theory.[2] According to Nederman, Oakley adopted a historical perspective based on the existence of continuity from the political and ecclesiological doctrines of conciliarists to modern constitutional theories. This perspective, Nederman notes, fails in its explanation of the distinction between "medieval" and "modern" cultures. Oakley took on the basic features of Figgis's interpretation of the genesis of modern political thought, and in doing so his position is ambiguous. In fact, speaking of conciliarism in terms of "constitutionalism," Oakley recognizes the "medieval character" of this movement, so that it seems contradictory to place it, at the same time, at the very origin of "modern" constitutional ideas.[3]

Nederman explains that Oakley—and Tierney with him—wrongly sees a continuity between fourteenth-century conciliarism and modern constitutionalism, ignoring the crucial cultural turn in the understanding of the natural and supernatural worlds that took place in the fifteenth and sixteenth centuries. The rise of a doctrine of "natural rights," like the one we find since the sixteenth century, is a crucial feature of modernity and is part of modern constitutional doctrines.[4] Natural rights, a constitutive element of modern European political culture, would have their origin not in the late Middle Ages but in the "linguistic turn" that occurred during the Renaissance.

Assuming certain basic elements of Quentin Skinner's perspective, with direct reference to *The Foundation of Modern Political Thought*, Nederman maintains that the crucial element that marks the change from one age to another is a shift in language.[5] On this perspective, the main limitation of Oakley's and Tierney's studies is precisely the idea of continuity. If historians focus mainly on the use of certain sets of words, notions, and expressions, as Oakley and Tierney do, this could move the analysis of the meaning of such phrases into the background. The fact that two authors use the same word does not mean that they understand that word in the same way. Therefore, according to Nederman's criticism, even if Grotius used the term *ius naturale*, as Ockham did, this does not mean that the two authors had the same semantic value in mind. On the basis of Skinner's study, Nederman denies the possibility of a common semantic background for authors so distant in time and culture: there is a radical difference between Ockham and Grotius, caused by the changes that occurred in the fifteenth and sixteenth centuries.[6] The rise of modernity left Ockham's doctrines in the medieval world, while Grotius's political and intellectual sensibility is fully part of the modern age. Between Ockham and Grotius, Nederman notes, stands what John Pocock called "the Machiavellian moment," which marks the beginning of "modernity" for political thought.[7]

Replying to Nederman, Oakley and Tierney reaffirm their belief in a long continuity as the basic feature of the history of natural rights and clarify the roles of certain important figures in the development of natural rights doctrines. The supporters of the idea of a radical or crucial turning point in natural rights theory place it in the writings of seventeenth-century theorists. In particular, Adam Seagrave recently provided an interpretation that highlights the innovative features of John Locke's political and legal doctrines.[8] Seagrave criticizes Tierney's interpretation and notes that Locke's *Two Treatises of Government* elaborated a natural rights theory that is not part of a long, continuous tradition. Even if it is true that the English seventeenth-century philosopher built his own theory on those of his predecessors, Seagrave remarks, Locke evidences a profound change in priority.[9] According to this interpretation, Locke's idea of natural rights represents a "Copernican moment" in legal and political history. This change, Seagrave notes, could hardly be explained from a continuity perspective like the one proposed by Tierney.[10]

In a certain sense, in Seagrave's critical remarks on Tierney we can see the concern with defining the specific and original features of modern political, moral, and legal thought. Thus Seagrave shares Nederman's intent. But while Nederman aims to present modern natural rights theory as a specific feature of modern political constitutionalism in order to preserve the "medieval" character of the political doctrines of Ockham and Gerson, Seagrave develops another suggestion taken directly from Leo Strauss's picture of the genesis of natural rights theory. According to Strauss, the English seventeenth-century political debate is the framework within which this theory arose. In particular, Thomas Hobbes and John Locke are seen as the true founders of the idea of human natural rights.[11] Seagrave, presenting Locke as the author of a radical new perspective on these issues, affirms, against Tierney and the supporters of the continuity thesis, the existence of a precise "birthdate" of modern political and moral culture.[12]

Nederman's and Seagrave's criticism certainly underestimates the value of continuity in the history of natural rights. But this "continuity" has to be understood as a process, not simply as a recurrence of similar formulas or lexicons. It is a process in which the expressions *ius naturale* and *lex naturalis* are debated, discussed, defined, and redefined by every author and according to fluid historical circumstances. If the distinction medieval/modern has to be made carefully so as not to understand it in an ideological way, then it is necessary at the same time to maintain the distinction between the features of the different historical "seasons."[13] In particular, Nederman directs attention to the need to recognize the importance of the changes that took place during the Renaissance. The cultural developments first in Italy and then in the rest of Europe between the fifteenth and sixteenth centuries cannot be underestimated. The changing perception and understanding of the notion of "nature" and of the order of the world, of the place of human beings, are crucial and profoundly influence the way in which the authors of this time read their predecessors' writings on natural law and natural rights. Sixteenth-century Thomists (Vitoria, Suárez, Vazquez) were well acquainted with the works of Aquinas, as well as with the natural rights medieval tradition, but they read these doctrines according to the cultural framework of their time.

## The Crucial Passages: Changes,
## Shifts, or Turning Points?

Central to Tierney's reading of the history of natural rights theory is the idea of a long shift of meaning or, better, of a plural development of a tradition of legal and moral thought, the roots of which are found in the works of the twelfth-century canonists. According to this perspective, the controversy about "Franciscan poverty," Ockham's political writings, conciliarism, sixteenth-century Thomism, and Grotius are not turning points but stages in a process, chapters in one and the same history. For Tierney, the theorists of natural rights associated with each one of these passages combine the originality that comes from their specific historical context with continuity, which depends on their belonging to a specific legal and moral culture.[14]

Recently, Francis Oakley and Annabel Brett both reaffirmed the need to emphasize the specific features of some of these passages with respect to the background of a *longue durée* and have expressed a general consensus on Tierney's historical approach. Oakley reaffirms the two main pillars of his interpretation in two volumes published in the beginning of the 2000s. In *The Conciliar Tradition* (2003), he develops the idea of basic continuity in the history of the conciliar tradition in Catholic Church history and strongly defends the thesis that precisely this tradition, which dates to the early thirteenth century, provided the basic notions and arguments for constitutionalism.[15] The growth of a "political" understanding of the church as "institution" started with the twelfth-century legal revival and created the cultural basis for the fourteenth-century development of a constitutional discourse inside the Catholic Church as a reaction to the ecclesiastical and political crisis of the Great Schism. For Oakley, the result of such a historical process was the rise of a "constitutional culture" inside the church that, on the one hand, created the basis for the successive secular theories and, on the other, gave rise to several developments inside the Catholic Church up to the Second Vatican Council and the ecclesiological doctrine of *Lumen gentium*.[16]

This renewal of attention to the "constitutional" character of conciliarism goes together with the new focus on the natural rights interpretation that Oakley has elaborated. In his *Natural Law, Laws of Nature, Natural Rights* (2005), he presents his view as based on one assumption and three arguments.[17] The assumption is that the distinction between the "medieval" and "modern" ages is quite problematic, if not a stumbling block, for a historical inquiry on *ius naturale* and *lex naturalis*. The English scholar clearly rejects Nederman's objections and criticisms and agrees with the perspective of historians such as Antony Black, Brian Tierney, and James H. Burns in considering the history of these ideas as a long shift from the twelfth to eighteenth centuries. The three arguments that Oakley develops concern (1) the ambiguity of the term *natura* in the last two millennia; (2) the crucial importance of the fourteenth-century turning point, shift, or discontinuity in the understanding "of both the nature of nature and the essence of law"; and (3) the influence of biblical commitments in the fourteenth-century shift from scholastic theology and philosophy.[18] Even if the fourteenth century marks the crucial milestone in the construction of thinking about modern rights, Oakley stresses his basic agreement with Tierney's argument in favor of a long evolutionary development of natural rights language and cultural features. This development essentially originated in "medieval jurisprudence," with eventual philosophical and theological interactions.[19]

Annabel Brett shares with Oakley the view that the fourteenth century has a crucial place in the history of modern natural rights theory.[20] In addition, she develops Quentin Skinner's idea that another crucial historical passage is represented by sixteenth-century scholasticism.[21] Brett also takes from Skinner a methodological element: analysis of the changes in language. According to Brett, in fact, the study of the use of terms like *ius*, *dominium*, and *potestas* guides the historical inquiry more accurately than the search for the origins of modern natural rights.[22] Thus she focuses on the careful identification of the double use of *ius* in terms of *facultas* or *potestas*, that is, subjective right as "objective" right. This leads Brett to move nominalism, voluntarism, and realism to the background and to focus on the nature of the texts in which *ius* has a "subjective" value.

Brett's aim is to provide the historical and cultural basis for an understanding of the doctrines of the school of Salamanca in sixteenth-century Spain.[23] Here again, she is moving from Skinner's account, according to which Vitoria, Soto, Vazquez, and other sixteenth-century Spanish scholastic thinkers elaborated the notion of subjective individual rights that is proper to the modern age and that, through Grotius, influenced John Locke.[24] Brett offers a picture of the different languages concerning natural rights, elaborated during the fourteenth and fifteenth centuries, as the background for the sixteenth-century discourse on "rights." At that moment Dominicans and Jesuits developed their own theories using the plural range of meanings, concepts, and ideas that late medieval traditions provided for them.[25]

## DOES METAPHYSICS HAVE A ROLE IN THE FOUNDATION OF NATURAL RIGHTS THEORY?

Tierney and Brett in their accounts of the history of natural rights place importance on careful study of language. For them, "natural law" and "natural rights" are phrases that properly belong to juridical and legal culture. This historical perspective leads Brett to put the metaphysical foundation of natural rights in the background and Tierney to consider it as not essential to the understanding of the history of this idea. The two scholars maintain this nonmetaphysical perspective particularly with respect to Ockham's theory of natural rights.

As I have already mentioned, for Tierney, Ockham's nominalism, as well as his voluntarism and individualism, had no crucial or significant influence on his account of natural rights.[26] The Venerabilis Inceptor would have considered the matter of natural law and natural rights from a legal and political point of view, as the use of a specific "juridical" language seems to suggest. In particular, as Tierney notes developing a remark made by Sten Gagnér, the

Franciscan master seems to have been acquainted with the canon-istic tradition.[27] His political writings show in fact several reliances on the contents of Gratian's *Decretum* and its interpreters and on the *Decretals* and canonistic tradition.[28] According to Tierney's reading, Ockham would have elaborated not just a new and revo-lutionary understanding of *ius naturale* in subjective terms on the basis of his nominalism and voluntarism, but he would have put a new emphasis on terms like *natura* and *ratio* as the sources of sub-jective rights.[29]

In addition, Brett supports an interpretation of Ockham's dis-course on natural law and natural rights as very different from the earlier Franciscan tradition on these issues. While the theologians and jurists of the Minor Friars had debated *ius naturale* with re-spect to the dispute about poverty, Ockham would have changed the focus to a more general political discourse, understanding *ius* in terms of *potestas* according to a voluntarist perspective, which did not consider the reference to God's will as basic as the Franciscans did.[30] In particular, Brett stresses the importance, in Ockham's per-spective, of the equivalence between *potestas* and *ratio*. Since for Ockham *ius* is a *potestas*, when he spoke of *potestas licita* he was speaking of a "right" that is conformed to right reason.[31]

This reading of natural rights history sees it primarily as a mat-ter of legal and juridical thought and identifies a specific cultural tradition that involves canonists, jurists, and political thinkers. This tradition would have developed a specific language, which was independent from theological and metaphysical concerns and fo-cused mainly on political and legal issues.

Other scholars have discussed the influence that changes in metaphysical doctrines have had on natural rights theories. The followers and heirs of Michel Villey's historical perspective, such as Michel Bastit in the beginning of the 1990s, still stressed the crucial importance of the history of metaphysical thought in order to un-derstand the development of natural rights discourse.[32] It is the way in which "things" (*res*) are seen that determines the kind of natu-ral law and natural rights ideas. As Bastit remarks, Aristotelian-Thomistic theory rests on a specific vision of the world order with a clear metaphysics that provides a particular relation between "things" and law.[33] According to this philosophical perspective, natural law reflects the metaphysical order of reality, so that to understand natural law means to understand the order of things. For Bastit, William of Ockham marked a break with this tradition through the affirmation of his idea of *ius* as individual power.[34] Ockham's discontinuity is mainly metaphysical, because the new understanding of *ius naturale* and *lex naturalis* is no more than the final result of the abandonment of a realist philosophical perspective in favor of a "nominalist orthodoxy." First Duns Scotus and, more extensively, Ockham created a new metaphysics and thus built on it a new legal and moral order.[35]

Arthur Stephen McGrade shares the idea that Ockham's account of natural rights deals with metaphysical issues. In his contribution to the *Cambridge Companion to Ockham* he looks at the Venerabilis Inceptor's texts on natural rights and highlights the problem of understanding how the ideas that (1) ethical and social norms can be determined rationally without reference to God's will, (2) all valid norms are divine commands, and (3) God can command virtually anything can be combined.[36] The point, for McGrade, is to explain the coherence of Ockham's notions of *lex naturalis* and *ius naturale* with the nominalist doctrine of God's absolute and ordained powers.

Oakley, in his last writings, also argues for the importance of the "nominalistic turn" in metaphysics to explain the development and evolution of natural rights theories. Oakley, following the same method as Tierney and Brett, notes that from the fourteenth to the sixteenth century a significant shift occurred in the concept of nature.[37] This shift, which started with the new nominalist philosophical perspective, leads to an idea of nature that then became proper to modern natural philosophy and science. What Oakley evidences is thus the crucial role of the construction of the scientific concept of nature and natural law.[38] This change in language and culture goes together with the historical process that led to modern natural rights. According to this understanding of the importance of the idea of *natura*, metaphysics are crucial to the development of legal and moral discourse. However, Oakley also issues two warnings: first, not all thinkers made their accounts of natural law and natural rights systematically; and second, their writings and ideas dealt with the limits and given conditions of the culture of their times.

The role of metaphysics in natural rights discourse remains a subject of debate. If it is true that the changes in metaphysical perspectives go together with the evolution and sequence of historical stages, then it is also clear that "natural law" and "natural rights" have progressively concerned mainly the legal and juridical order rather than the metaphysical. We can ask if the distinction between juridical and metaphysical discourse is constitutive of the discourse of natural law and natural rights or if it is just one of the aspects of its development since a precise moment.

The basic question is how different fields, such as philosophy, theology, and law, were connected and separated in various phases of the history of natural rights. This question requires a good understanding of the historical and cultural evolution of the notions of *theologia, philosophia, iurisprudentia,* and *scientia legis* at various cultural moments in the medieval and early modern periods. The idea that medieval cultures always rendered a systematic account can be misleading and offers a stereotypical, if not ideological, picture of the more complex and fluid situation of European culture between the twelfth and seventeenth centuries. At the same time it is true that, according to a medieval cultural perception, what the *sancti,* or Fathers of the church, and the *philosophi,* or ancient philosophers, provided in their writings was an organic idea of reality. The different masters and schools, starting from debate over certain issues or from analysis of an authoritative book, tried to build accounts of reality as holistically as possible.

## THE ROLE OF SECULAR CULTURE

The reconsideration of the cultural climate in which medieval theories of natural law and natural rights were developed suggests that we should evaluate the role of other kinds of discourses on these issues, not merely that of religion. Tierney, Brett, and Oakley but also Villey, Finnis, and the majority of scholars share the idea that *ius naturale* and *lex naturalis* are notions defined and debated primarily in the context of medieval religious culture. The idea that canonists originated the different meanings and uses of these lemmas, the crucial role of authors like Aquinas, Ockham, and Gerson, or movements as conciliarism—all of these understandings agree in considering the general issue "religious" in its origins and developments.

Natural law and natural rights were, in fact, also the subject of debate in civil law, particularly since the Justinian *Code* and *Digest* were taken as the basic legal textbooks at the end of the eleventh century. In a 1963 article devoted to the fortunes of the Stoic formula *natura id est Deus*, Tierney traces the line that joins civil lawyers and canonists on the issue of nature.[39] However, considering the chain of the origin of natural rights theory, he then focuses on the role of the canonists as creators of a new legal and juridical language. In the 1990s, Kenneth Pennington returned to the importance of civil lawyers in the history of natural law and natural rights.[40] He stressed in particular their role in mediating ancient Roman legal culture for the Middle Ages: their attention to the topic of "property" and their use of Roman sources are considered relevant for successive developments in legal theory. Among these developments, Pennington, following Tierney, highlights the crucial importance of the writings of the canonists.

Several scholars in the second half of the twentieth century have stressed the need to consider legists crucial for the definition of ideas such as natural law and natural rights. Ennio Cortese, in his 1962–64 two-volume work, *La norma giuridica*, presents an analysis of medieval civil law according to which *lex naturalis* and *ius naturale* are the ground of the entire science of law.[41] The collection of texts and documents published by Rudolf Weigand in his *Naturrechtslehere* (1967) also testifies to the importance of legists.[42] According to Weigand's perspective, natural law and natural rights were notions that belonged to the entire medieval legal culture, which they had inherited from ancient Roman tradition and from the Fathers of the Church. Even if the German scholar distinguishes between legists and decretists in his volume, he nevertheless juxta-poses Irnerius and Gratian, Accursius and Johannes Teutonicus, as figures belonging to the same cultural framework.

In recent decades, Italian scholars have developed this ap-proach, starting mainly from Francesco Calasso's works on the development of medieval legal culture and from Cortese's studies. They stressed the need for acquaintance with both the texts and the intellectual milieu of medieval natural law doctrines.[43] Paolo Grossi, in his *L'ordine giuridico medievale* ([1995] 2006), inserts civil law innovations of the so-called *età sapienziale del diritto* (wis-dom age of law), that is, the eleventh through thirteenth centuries, into a more general historical portrait of the late Middle Ages.[44] In particular, he stresses what he called *reicentrisimo*, the "centrality of things," as the main feature of medieval culture. It is precisely this central place that medieval authors bestowed to things that, for Grossi, is the core of medieval legal doctrine. According to him, *res*, and thus *natura*, is at the center of the process of construction of legal institutions, concepts, and practices and leads to the idea that law and right are mainly descriptions of an order already given in nature. *Res* entails *ordo*, and thus a clear rational structure of reality that law simply transposes in language. Natural law is not a will dependent on the decisions of the political ruler but the rational order inherent to nature that human beings, as rational creatures, can understand.[45] What the legists created is a juridical system that in twelfth-century Europe grew up together—and was often in competition—with canon law and ecclesiastical order.

The thought of legists on natural law and natural rights is in fact part of that "plurality" of juridical systems that characterized the late Middle Ages. At the same time, precisely these issues seem to have been the common ground of debate between legists and canonists since the twelfth century. Moreover, as Cortese shows, the founders of civil law in the eleventh-century Bolognese frame-work, such as Pepo and Irnerius, seem to have been deeply influ-enced by religious, biblical, and theological interests. Some sources, for instance, suggest that Pepo, in the middle of the eleventh cen-tury, was the first to assume that the content of natural law included in ancient Roman legislation was already present in the scriptures. Irnerius is the supposed author of a collection of theological sentences, mainly drawn from Augustine, the so-called *Liber divinarum sententiarum*.[46] A certain chronicle tradition also attests to the existence of a connection between the Bolognese legist and the French theological culture of the time. He was, in fact, identified as a disciple of Lanfranc of Bec. Certainly, as Andrea Padovani has noted, there was circulation of texts and men between the great schools of northern France and the masters of law in Bologna.[47] Irnerius's logical culture, in addition to his acquaintance with the Augustinian exegetical method proper to biblical studies, is a clue to the existence of such links. Further, the cases of masters of theology like the magister Albericus that John of Salisbury mentioned in his *Metalogicon*, who went from Paris to Bologna to study and teach law after an education in logic and philosophy, indicate that the twelfth-century European cultural framework was characterized by fluid disciplinary as well as territorial boundaries.[48]

Thus legists were a crucial component of the medieval Latin world. Their account of natural law and natural rights needs to be considered also for its influence on canonists and theologians. Irnerius and his intellectual heirs found these notions in the very beginning of the *Digest* and of the *Institutiones* and tried to understand them, as Padovani notes, by appealing to all the cultural sources at their disposal. In particular, they drew notions and methods from their philosophical knowledge. They largely used the set of notions and rules of ancient logic together with the moral and metaphysical heritage that came from the Stoic and Platonic traditions through the works of authors such as Boethius and Calcidius. At the same time they also drew from crucial aspects of the religious tradition to which they belonged, for instance, taking the basic rules for the exegesis of authoritative texts from the Augustinian heritage. According to Padovani's interpretation, the interest of the legists in a clear definition of the notion of *ordo naturae* together with their idea of the "religious" character of such order were the basis for their positions on the notions of *ius naturale* and *lex naturalis*.[49]

*Chapter 5*

# HIGHLIGHTS AND
# SHADOWS OF A
# PORTRAIT

Having considered the most significant scientific studies on the origins of modern natural rights doctrine produced since the 1950s, it is possible to summarize their conclusions. Authors like Villey, Tuck, Oakley, and Tierney certainly share an interest in the medieval origins of modern natural rights doctrines and consider the writings of late medieval canonists and theologians either as the background for understanding modern developments or as a break with the objective idea of *ius naturae* or as a long and complex shift. The interpretations that Villey and Tierney develop rest on the basic assumption that a cornerstone of modern political as well as ethical thought has its roots in the cultural, political, and religious dynamics of Europe between the twelfth and fifteenth centuries.[1] On the other hand, the simple juxtaposition of the various interpretations shows the differences that exist between scholars, and thus we need to identify and define disagreements and unresolved matters. This kind of double evaluation, which combines the well-illumined characteristics of the medieval idea of *lex naturae* and *ius naturae* with the many obscure and unclear aspects of its history will lead to a reconsideration of the preliminary problem of the scientific method to be employed in such research. As a matter of history of ideas or history of concepts, does the inquiry into natural law and natural rights belong to historians or philosophers, to theologians or jurists?

## THE SKETCH OF A PORTRAIT

Medieval authors inherited the terms *lex naturae* (or *naturalis*) and *ius naturae* (or *naturale*) from ancient Roman legal culture, both directly, through Justinian's collection of laws and jurisprudence, and indirectly, through the medium of the Fathers of the Church. The latter, most notably Isidore of Seville, used in their writings the concepts of Roman legal tradition to produce a series of definitions and syntheses that were the starting point for many medieval authors. What began in Latin Western Europe at the end of the eleventh century is a cultural process within which a variegated and articulated moral and legal lexicon would develop. Medieval authors, in the general framework of the political and ecclesiastical conflicts between the papacy and the empire and, more generally, between religious and secular authorities, turned back to the idea of general universal natural rules, which ground the values of a legal order. In the opening words of the *Digest*, a quotation from Ulpian describes natural law as the principle that is common to men and animals and rules all living beings.

> Natural law is that which all animals have been taught by nature; this law is not peculiar to the human species, it is common to all animals which live on land or sea, and to fowl of the air as well. From it comes the union of man and woman, called matrimony by us, and therewith the procreation and rearing of children; we find in fact that animals in general, the very wild beasts, are marked by acquaintance with this law.[2]

Canon lawyers, such as Irnerius, followed the words of the *Digest* and understood natural law as the basic rule of creation. Natural law is something that pertains to every living being and thus is something that has no private dimension.[3] According to Irnerius,

*ius naturale* is thus the basic order of the world, which allows every animal, including human beings, to generate and to socialize.[4] *Natura* and *naturalis* refer here to the basic order that God established and through which he taught his creatures how to accomplish their duty within creation.[5]

Since Irnerius and his successors seem to combine the letter of the Roman law with the Christian idea of creation as order, which is a means of divine revelation (see Rom. 2:13), they support this cultural process also under the influence of Calcidius's reading of Plato's *Timaeus*; from that they take the idea of *lex naturalis* or *ius naturale* to indicate the natural condition of all living things, the natural order that human laws and hierarchies try to imitate. Such a perspective is well summarized by the anonymous author of the *Summa institutionum Vindobonensis*.

> Natural law is the condition that is imposed upon created things according to the very divine disposition, or it is the natural instinct, which is not established by something else. For it is established not by human activity, but by divine disposition. Nature, in fact, teaches this law to all the animals and all the animals are qualified by the ability of this law. The union between male and female, which we call, with some solemnity, marriage, comes from it. The generation and education of sons comes from it. All of these things are not called laws but effects of the law.[6]

*Ius naturale* became the name used to indicate the general condition or the general order established by God's will within which a set of rules is possible. It is a sort of "genus" of which human law (*ius gentium*) is a species. As Martinus clearly explains: "Natural law, on one hand, is generic and concerns all animals, on the other hand, it is a species and concerns only human beings and is also called *ius gentium*."[7] "Law" (*ius*), following Celsius's definition, is the "art of good and equity" and the proper definition of different kinds of prescriptive orders: the order of nature, which divine will establishes; and the human order, which human reason establishes.[8]

What emerges is clearly the scheme of an order where human law, that is, the *ius gentium*, is defined as a species of the genre of natural law. Human law is, in fact, that specific kind of natural law which is proper to human beings as rational creatures.

According to several scholars, civil law contributed to the reintroduction of "natural law" to the intellectual debate.[9] However, as historians like Harold Berman, Brian Tierney, Paolo Prodi, and Diego Quaglioni have stressed, canonists were the authors of the most significant turning point in the history of this idea of natural law.[10] Their engagement in the construction of a new legal order, that is, canon law, which Berman calls the papal revolution, changed radically the concept of *ius naturale* with respect to the heritage of Roman legal culture and to the ideas of eleventh- and twelfth-century legists. Gratian, with the double definition of *ius naturale* given in his *Decretum*, reorganized previous ideas and elements and established the basis for the development of a series of theories of *ius naturale*. He first explains:

> The human race is ruled by two things, namely by natural law and usages. Natural law is what is contained in the Law and the Gospel. By it, each person is commanded to do to others what he wants done to himself and prohibited from inflicting on others what he does not want done to himself.[11]

Then Gratian offered a different definition:

> Natural law is common to all nations because it exists everywhere through natural instinct, not because of any enactment. For example: the union of men and women, the succession and rearing of children, the common possession of all things, the identical liberty of all, or the acquisition of things that are taken from the heavens, earth, or sea, as well as the return of a thing deposited or of money entrusted to one, and repelling of violence by force. This, and anything similar, is never regarded as unjust but is held to be natural and equitable.[12]

The two texts, both present in the *Decretum*, show clearly that Gratian was aware of the existence of different perspectives on natural law. According to the first definition, *ius naturale* is basically a moral principle, the so-called Golden Rule of scripture, both the Old Testament (Tobit 4:16) and the Gospels (Matt. 7:12). By contrast, the second definition appears to be a reelaboration of the basic concepts in the Roman legal heritage. Here in fact natural law is identified with human law, the law common to all peoples, or *ius gentium*. This law maintains that a natural instinct rules the biological life of human beings and animals. The use of this definition of *ius naturale* suggests that Gratian, like all the subsequent canonists, was quite well acquainted with the content of the legal culture of his time. He was clearly aware of the fact that the legists saw natural law as the order of creation established by God, that is, a principle of "good and equity," that would be the model for human law. For Irnerius, Martinus, and the other civil lawyers, *ius naturale* was the expression of the divine *aequitas* in ruling creation, and this *aequitas* was the perfect model for the establishment of human law. Human reason has to exercise *aequitas* according to the model of divine *aequitas* and in this way can establish the *ius gentium* that is her own creation.[13]

With respect to this "Platonic" model, where natural law and divine *aequitas* are the paradigm for *ius gentium* and human *aequitas*, canonists changed the basic elements of the discourse.[14] Natural law is something proper to human beings only, because it is something that can be understood only by rational creatures. Thus *ius naturale* is not just a model; it is a normative principle on which reason can ground all positive laws. In his second definition of *ius naturale*, Gratian assumes this perspective. Even if he uses the elements of Roman legal tradition, the identification of *ius naturale* and *ius gentium* puts the former in the exclusively human sphere. It is no more a matter of natural order: *ius naturale* is a matter of human reason.

The evolution of the notions of *lex naturae* and *ius naturae* from the eleventh to the twelfth century suggests also the existence of a close relationship between the legal and religious cultures. Meanwhile, Irnerius and Pepo devoted their attention to Roman law, finding the terms *ius naturale* and *lex naturalis* in crucial biblical passages, mainly in Paul's Epistle to the Romans and its ancient interpretations. The early twelfth-century exegetes, such as Anselm of Laon, William of Champeaux, and Peter Abelard and their disciples, developed the concept of natural law starting from this idea:

> For not the hearers of the law are just before God, but the doers of the law shall be justified. For when the Gentiles, who do not have the law, do by nature those things that are of the law; these having not the law are a law to themselves: Who shew the work of the law written in their hearts, their conscience bearing witness to them, and their thoughts between themselves accusing, or also defending one another.[15]

They also reflected on the relation between law and authority starting from the idea:

> Let every soul be subject to higher powers: for there is no power but from God: and those that are, are ordained of God. Therefore he that resisteth the power, resisteth the ordinance of God. And they that resist, purchase for themselves damnation. For princes are not a terror to the good work, but to the evil.[16]

Martin Grabmann, Joseph De Ghellinck, Odon Lottin, David Luscombe, and, more recently, Antonio Padovani and Cédric Giraud have studied the contribution that these theological schools made to the assumption of natural law and natural rights as the basic ideas of medieval moral and legal discourses.[17] Thanks to the new schools that grew up in the main European cities or along with the major cathedrals and abbeys of the time, these doctrines quickly became part of the common cultural background. It is, in fact, clear that these schools served as a network in Latin Europe within which writings and ideas circulated.

Gratian's supposed connection with the Parisian theological framework, in particular, with Peter Abelard's writings, ideas, and method, is certainly a legend, but, as Padovani stresses, it rests on the real link between twelfth-century Parisian schools and their contemporaries in Bologna. The way in which Gratian selected and collected the patristic *auctoritates* and the juridical texts of the church tradition is an exemplary product of early twelfth-century scholastic culture. At the same time the *Decretum* marks the beginning of a disciplinary distinction between theological and legal discourses, which Stephen of Tournai (1128–1203) clearly explains in the prologue to his *Summa* on Gratian's text.[18] Furthermore, when Stephen composed his *Summa*, Peter Lombard had already completed his *Sententiae* and his commentaries to the Psalms and the Pauline epistles, using as a source the *Glossa ordinaria* and providing texts which became influential in the following decades.

Therefore twelfth-century authors considered *ius naturale* and *lex naturalis* from a theological and exegetical perspective, as well as from a legal and philosophical one. This plurality suggests that the development of the different doctrines has to be placed against the background of the rising of medieval "scholasticism" and of the formation of the great cultural traditions in philosophy, theology, and civil and canon law.[19] At the same time, these various cultures were linked with the new pastoral care that was at the center of the decrees of the Third Lateran Council (1179).[20] The religious and political evolution of the European framework stimulated the development of two different discourses: the theological one, devoted to the clarification of the boundaries and features of the orthodox faith; and the legal one, which concerns the construction of the ecclesiastical legal order and the definition of the institutional structure of the church.

## MORAL ORDER VERSUS LEGAL ORDER

Medieval authors began to distinguish between the moral and legal orders, insofar as they stressed a clear difference between sin and crime. As many scholars have noted, the twelfth century marks the beginning of what Colin Morris called "the discovery of the individual."[21] Peter Abelard seems to be the first author to clearly establish this distinction. Starting from the epistles of Saint Paul, the master evidences the inadequacy of a legal system that identifies crime with sinful action. Abelard, following the heritage of the biblical exegesis of the school of Laon, particularly with respect to the second chapter of the Epistle to the Romans, develops a critique of a certain meaning of law.[22] Sin and crime are two different things, and they cannot be subject to the same kind of prescription. In fact, if a crime is a wrong action, a sin is a wrong action motivated by a wrong or sinful intention. Abelard seems conscious of the need to distinguish the two things and at the same time to include them in the same order. Therefore, the point is how to establish an objective parameter for evaluating whether the agent's intention is good or evil. Abelard makes the distinction between *ius naturale* and *ius positivum*.

> One sort of law is called "natural," the other "positive." Natural law is what the reason naturally innate in all people urges should be put into effect, and therefore remains the same among all people: such as, to worship God, to love one's parents, to punish the wicked, and to do whatever is necessary in the sense that without them no other merits whatever will be sufficient. To positive justice, however, belongs what is set up by humans so as to preserve usefulness and worth more safely and increase them. It rests either on custom alone or on written authority.[23]

The master suggests that a good intention is one conforming to the dictate of divine will and this divine will is nothing more than the content of *ius naturale*, that is, natural law that human reason is able to know without revelation. This "natural law" is the first law and coincides with the knowledge of moral principles and precepts.

According to this perspective, *ius naturale* is the basis for the reconciliation between the field of sin and the field of crime, that is, between the legal and moral order, insofar as it is the parameter for evaluating the right intention and thus the goodness of the subsequent action. *Ius naturale* becomes the God-given ground of a Christian ethics. In fact, according to Abelard's texts, even if "natural law" is not sufficient for salvation, it allows each human being to know and love God and thus to live a good life because it determines the relation between intention and moral value of the action.[24] On the contrary, "human law," that is, positive law, has a more social value, insofar as it concerns the relation between crime and punishment.

Abelard's distinction between the sphere of morality and the sphere of law is parallel to the rise of a distinction between the activity of canon lawyers and that of masters of the sacred page. All these intellectuals developed different cultural perspectives even if they dealt with the same subject, *ius naturale*: Irnerius and his disciples looked to this topic when they considered the letter of the *Digest* and of the *Institutiones*, while Anselm of Laon and his pupils started from the verses of Holy Scripture. These two traditions developed throughout the twelfth century, in a cultural process within which they influenced each other and considered the contemporary discussions among canonists. Finally, these authors produced summaries of their positions both in the *Glossa ordinaria* to the *Digest* and in the *Glossa ordinaria* to scripture.

Accursius, in the *Glossa* to the beginning of the *Institutiones*, shows a clear consciousness of the various perspectives on *ius naturale*: the laws of Moses and the Gospels, the natural instinct, the *ius gentium*, and the *ius pretorium*.[25] Even if conscious of the different definitions of *ius naturale*, Accursius stressed the fact that legists still considered natural law the basic order of creation, that is, that *aequitas* which is common to all living things and upon which rests the entire legal order.[26] If we turn to the glosses to Romans 2:14, which are an abridgement of Peter Lombard's notes to Paul's epistles, natural law is presented as that universal rule given by God, which is available to all rational beings and which allows them to distinguish good and evil.[27] Natural law is thus something that pertains to human beings as rational, and is not shared with other kinds of living beings. What Paul describes as *lex naturalis* is a moral principle rather than the basis of a legal order. The capacity to distinguish good and evil through rational judgment is proper to human beings: it is the feature of the condition of human beings after the fall. Human beings are capable of discerning good and evil but are not capable, by nature alone, of acting well and saving themselves. This is possible only by the action of divine grace.

When Gratian composed his *Concordantia Discordantium Canonum*, he was clearly aware of the existence of these two cultural "traditions," which, in a certain sense, continue with Peter Abelard's distinction between morality and legal order. The two definitions of *ius naturale* that Gratian offered seem an attempt to assimilate Roman legal tradition and the fruits of biblical exegesis in a new legal order. This suggests that, as Kenneth Pennington recently noted, for what concerns the idea of *ius naturale*, starting from Gratian, canon law can be seen also as a construction that tries to combine that which comes from legal and biblical cultures.[28] Huguccio of Pisa, in his account of *ius naturale*, juxtaposes several definitions that concern moral life as well as legal order. In particular, it is clear that he assumes some basic elements of the notion of *ius naturale* that Abelard had stressed and Gratian had also assumed: the identity of "natural law" and "divine law" and the idea that the very content of *ius naturale* is the Golden Rule: "All things therefore whatsoever you would that men should do to you, do you also to them" (Matt. 7:12).[29]

These two features put the matter of the foundation of both the legal and moral orders in the theological field, which in the first decades of the thirteenth century was becoming a specific discipline. This created the condition for the development of a theological debate concerning the idea of "law," the order among the different kinds of "laws," and the status of *ius naturale* within this order. Theologians, in fact, appear quite concerned with the need for a stable foundation of moral life as well as for a stable foundation for the authority of the different institutions. John of La Rochelle's *De legibus*, whose contents were reproduced in the *Summa fratris Alexandri*, Albert the Great's *Summa de creaturis*, and Peter of

Tarantaise's *Quaestiones de legibus* all aim to ground the ideas of *ius naturale* and *lex naturalis* within theological discourse.

## METAPHYSICAL ROOTS

One of the great points of debate among contemporary scholars concerns the relationship between moral and political discourse and metaphysical discourse in the building of natural law doctrines. Tierney's account questions the existence of a basic link between moral and political analysis on the one hand and metaphysics on the other. According to Villey and his disciples, Aquinas's theory of *ius naturale* is the result of a historical and cultural process that, through the progressive acquisition of the metaphysical content of Aristotelian philosophy, grounded the moral and political discourse in a specific understanding of the world order. The radical break caused by Ockham in the first decades of the fourteenth century was thus basically a break from Aquinas's understanding of the world order. Ockham, varying from Duns Scotus's realism, radically changed the metaphysical perspective by promoting nominalism. Precisely on the basis of his nominalism, he built his own doctrine of *ius naturale* as a subjective right, that is, a power or faculty proper to every individual human being.

Francis Oakley supports the idea that the beginning of modern rights theory, that is, the understanding of *ius naturale* as referring to the features of individual human beings, has to be placed in correspondence with the radical shift from thirteenth-century realism to fourteenth-century nominalism. According to Oakley, the construction of the basic features of modern natural rights theory by fourteenth-century conciliarists rests on the new nominalistic metaphysics.

Brian Tierney has a different understanding of the history of natural law and natural rights theories, stressing the importance of the formation of a "legal tradition" with a specific technical language, forged in the debate of the decretists. This language was taken up by subsequent natural law and natural rights theorists.

According to this interpretation, metaphysics does not have the crucial role that both Villey and Oakley suggest. Tierney notes, in fact, that William of Ockham's political writings do not show any explicit link with his radical nominalism.

The different opinions concerning the role of metaphysics as the foundation of natural law and natural rights discourse offer useful elements for reconsidering the history of *ius naturale*. As Tierney shows, twelfth-century canonists are the creators of a specific language concerning natural law and natural rights. This language became part of the common cultural background both in universities and in the offices of the papal curia and among high clergy. It is the language adopted for all subsequent discussions on natural law and natural rights. At the same time, even if *ius naturale* started off as the subject of canonistic inquiries, it has to be stressed that it was also the subject of other kinds of "scientific inquiries," like exegesis and theology, as well as philosophy. Moreover, use of a specific "legal" language of *ius naturale* does not mean that the understanding of this concept has no metaphysical implications.

In order to reconsider the matter of the possible metaphysical roots of the discourse on *ius naturale* it is useful to ask, what does "metaphysical" mean here? The word *metaphysics* has several meanings, and today it is commonly used to indicate "an attempt to describe the ultimate reality."[30] This idea, which arose in the early seventeenth century and particularly in Christian Wolff's *Metaphysics*, is proper to contemporary philosophical culture and is quite different from the medieval understanding of *metaphysica* as a part of philosophical knowledge.

In the Aristotelian scientific and philosophical account, medieval authors found the definition of a science of being qua being and of a science of the first cause, which was called *metaphysica* or *philosophia prima* (first philosophy). This definition became common in late medieval culture from the last decades of the twelfth century, thanks to the circulation of the Latin translations of Aristotle's *Metaphysics* and Avicenna's *Metaphysics*. According to this perspective, "metaphysics" means a kind of knowledge of the basic principles of the world order, principles that are available to human reason. The certainty that a world order exists given by God, which human beings, qua rational, could know and understand, is proper to the different seasons of medieval culture and is something that was already clearly evident in the glosses of the first legists in the eleventh and twelfth centuries. This kind of "metaphysical" vision influenced the understanding of the basic idea of "nature," which in twelfth-century culture is seen as the world order that is the sign of divine nature and grace.[31]

As mentioned above, in the decades at the turn of the twelfth century, the idea of nature as creation, which was clearly proper to biblical culture, was reconsidered in the light of Calcidius's commentary on Plato's *Timaeus* and the writings of John Scotus Eriugena.[32] Legists, as well as other authors of this period, used these sources to develop the idea of a God-given world order, namely, natural law, which is a model of perfect "equity" for the human positive legal order. This idea of an inner order of the world permeated medieval culture and was also shared by canonists and commentators on scripture. The formula *natura id est Deus*, which started to be used by both legists and canonists, summarized this sort of *Weltanschauung*, which supported the idea that the order of creation has a paradigmatic value for the moral and political order of human beings.[33]

Since the end of the twelfth century, the "Platonic" understanding of nature/creation began to be placed alongside that of a new philosophical tradition.[34] The increasing circulation of the Latin translation of several philosophical writings, mainly those of Aristotle, marked a radical change in the understanding of "metaphysics" as well as in the understanding of the idea of "nature." The Aristotelian corpus introduced the idea that "nature" could mean "the genesis of growing things" but also the cause of the growing process of things and the "essence" of things.[35]

The rise of this new perspective coincides with the significant epistemological development of different sciences and disciplines.

This cultural process, whose roots were already present in twelfth-century culture, rapidly increased with the rise of the university and with the assumption of the ideal of science taken from Aristotle's *Posterior Analytics*. Theology, medicine, civil law, and canon law are clearly defined according to their own principles. These changes in the basic set of ideas and knowledge and in the epistemological consciousness of the different disciplines influenced the approach to *ius naturale*. It is in fact in this period that masters of the arts and theologians began to criticize legists and canonists, claiming that "law," and thus also "natural law," is not a matter for legal studies but rather for philosophy, if not theology.[36]

The general context in which this cultural change happened is marked by what Leonard Boyle called "pastoral care."[37] What we find in the writings of masters of the arts, canonists, and masters in the sacred page is the development of a language that depends on the situations and events where the relation between law, authority, and moral responsibility is in question. Since the pontificate of Alexander III and particularly since the decrees of the Third Lateran Council, ecclesiastical policies focused on the government of the daily life of the church. In particular, the regulation of the sacraments assumed central relevance in the decisions and initiatives of the ecclesiastical authorities. The large part that the definition of ecclesiastical authority and sacraments plays in Gratian's *Decretum* and in Peter Lombard's *Sententiae* testifies to the relevance of these issues and their role in orienting legal and theological debate.

This new plural perspective concerning natural law and natural rights was clearly proper to theologians like Thomas Aquinas, whose aim was to offer systematic expositions of the notion of *ius naturale* in their *summae* and *quaestiones*. Jan Aertsen, in his studies on the thirteenth-century metaphysical doctrine of transcendentals, has underlined several times how it established an inseparable relation between ethics and metaphysics.[38] Aertsen notes that especially Thomas Aquinas used the transcendentals as the foundation of his theory of *lex naturalis*. The Dutch scholar suggests that some thirteenth-century authors did consider the ethical and political discourse on natural law as part of a larger and harmonious presentation of the world order. The same interest, however, was shared by the masters of the arts, whose teaching and thought was closely connected with lectures on and discussions of the Aristotelian texts.[39]

Eugenio Randi and most recently Luca Bianchi have considered the importance of the 1277 Parisian condemnations of philosophical doctrines in the rise of a new cultural perspective that also concerned natural law and natural rights.[40] Randi and Bianchi note the importance of the theological and metaphysical implications of the initiative of the archbishop of Paris, Étienne Tampier. The list of articles he condemned suggests an understanding of *philosophia* as a complete system of knowledge, where ethics, physics, and metaphysics are part of a comprehensive discourse. According to this perspective, natural law would not be independent from the metaphysical vision. The bishop chose some remarkable masters and theologians as members of the episcopal commission charged to examine the various doctrines.[41] Among them there was Henry of Ghent, the same master that Tierney has presented as one of the heirs of the canonistic tradition on natural law and natural rights. This circumstance links the 1277 condemnation with the rise of the nominalistic perspective on *lex naturalis* and *ius naturale*.

The rise of nominalism clearly marks a change in this cultural panorama. Its effects on the discourse on *ius naturale* were linked to those caused by the clash over apostolic poverty and its political and ecclesiastical consequences.[42] Scholars such as Marino Damiata and Roberto Lambertini have shown how the struggle between the two Franciscan parties and the intervention of the papacy can be seen as a laboratory for new arguments and theories concerning natural law and natural rights.[43] Moreover, several studies have stressed that, in addition to the *querelle* on apostolic poverty, the early fourteenth-century authors questioned the opposition between religious and secular power. First the fight between Boniface VIII and Philip the Fair of France and then the last attempts to restore the imperial universal authority stimulated the discussion about the properties and boundaries of both secular and ecclesiastical *potestates*.

In this context, the fact that Ockham assumed the lexicon of twelfth-century canonists does not contradict the fact that he had a clear consciousness that his theological and philosophical positions involved a new metaphysical basis for *ius naturale* and thus a rethinking of this concept. McGrade and other scholars have shown that in his theological and philosophical writings Ockham also debated natural law and natural rights.[44] His nominalism, in which he stressed the need to preserve God's omnipotence, guided him to a new account of *ius naturale*, as something established by divine will and as a power proper to every rational being.

This interest in natural law and natural rights in Ockham's theological writings is not in contradiction to the political perspective that characterized his writings on the occasion of the controversy with the papacy. Tierney's remark that Ockham here made use of the "legal" technical language, without any need for reference to the metaphysical foundations of the discourse on natural law and natural rights, does not imply that he considered the issue of *ius naturale* only a political and legal matter. It is clear that Ockham, questioning John XXII's arguments about poverty, papal power, and ecclesiology, decided to use the same kind of language and conceptual instruments that his opponent did—those of canon law. His account of natural law and natural rights in writings like the *Opus nonaginta dierum* or the *Dialogus* is thus certainly developed with the intellectual weapons of the reelaboration of an understanding of *ius naturale* in a subjective sense, which was already elaborated by authors such as Rufinus, Stephen of Tournai, and Huguccio.[45] But this doctrine is perfectly coherent with the metaphysical nominalism of his theological and philosophical writings. This explains how his doctrines could be transmitted to successive generations of natural law and natural rights theorists. It is in this sense that the contents of Ockham's discourse were inherited by many conciliarists, such as Gerson, and were also debated by authors of the different theological and philosophical traditions of the fourteenth and fifteenth centuries.

## OBJECTIVITY VERSUS SUBJECTIVITY

Studies have shown the existence of a distinction between the understanding of *ius naturale* as objective rule, that is, as synonymous with *lex naturalis*, and as subjective power of individuals. These two aspects involve the necessity of considering the development of the discourse of natural law and natural rights bearing in mind, on one side, the relation between *ius naturale* and authority and, on the other side, that of *ius naturale* and subjectivity.

*Ius naturale*, as a general rule to which positive law must conform, is synonymous with *lex naturalis*, natural law. In this sense, it represents a limit to all public authority. The papacy and canon lawyers presented it as the limit to the absolute power of the emperor and as the criterion for establishing the validity of every kind of positive law. *Ius naturale* as a power involves the definition of the specific psychological and moral features of human beings. In particular, it indicates the rational capacity to act well and to know and distinguish what is good and what is right (*synderesis*).

The distinction shows the links between natural law and natural rights doctrines and the development of moral and political thought. Canonists in the twelfth century used *ius naturale* in both senses. Huguccio writes in his *Summa*:

> Natural *ius* is called reason, namely a natural force of the soul with which a man can distinguish good and evil, choosing good and rejecting evil. . . . In a second sense, natural *ius* is called rational judgment, i.e., a movement which comes, directly or indirectly, from reason. . . . Thirdly, natural *ius* is called a natural instinct and a natural order. . . . In a fourth sense, natural *ius* is the divine *ius* because it is contained in the Law of Moses and in the Gospels. . . . Note that some say that there is a fifth meaning of this *ius*[,] . . . i.e., that all that is licit is approved, so that it is neither prescribed nor prohibited.[46]

Huguccio's first definition clearly has a subjective value. *Ius naturale*, in fact, corresponds to practical reason in its capacity to know the first principle of moral life: the capacity to distinguish good and evil, or *synderesis*. In addition, the idea that *ius naturale* can mean rational judgment involves a subjective perspective. Huguccio's position is coherent with a cultural background where the great scholastic masters elaborated their ideas and doctrines. Among these authors, in the middle decades of the thirteenth century, Thomas Aquinas has a crucial place because of his influence on subsequent masters.

The Dominican master uses *ius naturale* in the "political" field of the order of rules, that is, as *lex naturalis*, in a sense that is not in contradiction to a subjective theory of natural rights. Moreover, Aquinas, in his commentary to Aristotle's *Nicomachean Ethics*, shows knowledge of the tradition that understand *ius naturale* in terms of individual power. Commenting on a passage of the fifth book of Aristotle's work, he notes:

> We have then to consider that natural law is that to which human nature inclines. In man, there are two natures: one, which he shares with animals, according to which he is an animal; another one, which is proper to him inasmuch as he is a human being, which is human nature and which allows him to discern good and evil according to rationality. But jurists say that natural law is only the inclination which is common to humans and animals, such as the union between male and female, the care for children, and things like these; otherwise they called *ius gentium* (i.e., law of nations) that law which concerns the inclination proper to human nature, i.e., a human being as a rational animal, such as "respect the agreements," "protect ambassadors also among the enemies," and other similar things. However, Aristotle includes both of these types of natural law in the category of the "natural law."[47]

The fact that objective and subjective understandings of *ius naturale* are present in the writings of the same medieval author suggests a reconsideration of the opposition between natural law and natural rights. This opposition seems to be more present in recent times than in the Middle Ages. The debate about the preeminence of a universal set of rules (natural law), which God inscribed in human nature and on human rights (i.e., natural rights) as features of each individual human being, marks the polemical confrontation between significant parts of modern Catholic culture and political modernity, especially liberalism.

For medieval authors, natural law did not comprise a list of rules immediately and directly applicable to contingent circumstances.[48] On the contrary, natural law had a more general value: it appeared to be a sort of general legal and moral principle to which the human mind has to look in order to establish both the rules for ordinary life and the precepts for individual actions. The rise of a distinction between objectivity and subjectivity started only in the sixteenth century, when natural law became the foundation of modern state theories and natural rights were assumed as the powers and features of each individual human being. The idea that the passage from objectivity to subjectivity characterizes the history of natural law and natural rights is mainly a matter of contemporary historiography rather than of history. The duality subjective/objective, which is proper to modern and contemporary culture, is used to analyze the doctrinal debates of the late Middle Ages, when such a distinction seems to have a completely different value. A close examination of medieval texts reveals that the history of the ideas of natural law and natural rights seems more complex: at the end of the eleventh century canonists, jurists, biblical exegetes, and theologians discovered the semantic richness of these lemmas.

Brian Tierney clearly stresses in his studies how medieval authors used *lex naturalis* and *ius naturale* in various senses. In his recent study *Liberty and Law*, the American scholar notes that the twelfth-century canonists and the Parisian masters in theology are at the origin of the distinction between preceptive and permissive natural law.[49] It is this kind of distinction that is more proper to medieval men, whose interest is to define *lex* and *ius* and what kind of relation nature has with human action and with the legitimate exercise of power and authority.

# CONCLUSION

The studies analyzed above take distinctive points of view or are based on distinctive cultural premises, for example, the basic link between the rise and development of the discourse about *ius natu-rale* and the history of the church and its institutions. This would suggest an underestimation of the crucial contribution of civil law-yers and Roman legal heritage and of the philosophical culture that arose in the eleventh and twelfth centuries.

One element common to the historical approaches is the re-turn to the medieval roots of modern theories of natural law and natural rights. They begin with the contemporary understanding of these concepts. Both Villey and Tierney, for example, are concerned with how and when *ius naturale* started to be used in the sense of a subjective power proper to the nature of each individual human being. At the same time, the historical approaches all considered the plurality of meanings of *ius naturale*. This semantic richness was clearly and explicitly shown by the decretists, such as Huguccio, and assumed by all the great theorists of natural law and natural rights in the late Middle Ages. Thus it is necessary to evaluate the way in which these different meanings of *ius*—as a power, a faculty, or a rule—not only coexist in the same cultural context between the twelfth and sixteenth centuries but also were used together and influenced each other.

Historical studies on natural law and natural rights direct a strong critique at the philosophical analysis of medieval doctrines of natural law and natural rights. This is the case with Tierney's remarks on Finnis's presentation of Thomas Aquinas. According to Tierney, Finnis clearly showed that Aquinas's doctrine of natural law is perfectly compatible with a theory of subjective natural rights, even if there is no trace of the use in his writings of *ius* as a subjective natural right.

The limits of a purely philosophical approach "à la Finnis" do not necessarily involve a rejection or an underestimation of the contribution that a philosophical analysis can make to the history of *ius naturale* doctrines. A philosophical examination is in fact useful for evaluating the coherence of the reasoning in the legal and moral system to which these doctrines belong. Moreover, a philosophical evaluation can show clearly not only aspects of the meaning of *ius naturale* but also the potentialities of a doctrine, theory, or system of values and thus it can clarify developments in the history of ideas. The fact, which Finnis showed, that, for instance, Aquinas's account is in accord with a theory of *ius naturale* as a subjective power certainly helps us understand the philosophical basis on which a Thomist discourse concerning natural rights rests.

Similarly, theological analysis can assist historians of medieval doctrines of natural law and natural rights. "Natural law" and "natural rights" are matters proper not just to the legal tradition. They have been debated throughout the centuries by philosophers and theologians, whose work has influenced the debate and the development of new doctrines and accounts of these issues.[1] It is thus necessary for the historian to take a broad view of natural law and natural rights.

Together with these methodologies, scientific research needs to consider the existence of a connection between the evolution of historical events and changing notions of natural law and natural rights. The twelfth-century definition of these notions has to be evaluated within the framework of the so-called long twelfth century, from the decades of the investiture controversy to the pontificate of Innocent III, a century that includes the "renaissance" in art and culture.[2] The political, economic, social, and religious dynamics of this period led to the need for new legal, philosophical, and theological paradigms with which the men of that time could understand and order their world. Within the conflict between the royal or imperial powers and the religious *auctoritas* of the church, particularly the papacy, *lex naturalis* and *ius naturale* became powerful conceptual instruments. Legists used them to describe the natural condition of living beings with respect to which stands the imperial authority as the supreme source of order for human beings.[3] On the contrary, canonists underline the rationality of natural law and used *ius naturale* to indicate a power proper to human nature and in doing so set limits on positive law and political power.[4]

Events in the early decades of the thirteenth century prepared the way for the reception into European culture of Aristotelian thought, whose major consequence for natural law theories was Thomas Aquinas's doctrine according to which *lex naturalis* is the participation of human reason in the eternal divine law. The reaction against this position, commonly identified with fourteenth-century nominalists, started when Aquinas was still alive. Tampier's condemnations of 1270 and 1277, which involved certain Thomist principles, aimed, among other things, to reaffirm God's absolute power over all natural boundaries and to stress the "divine" origin of natural law.[5]

Starting from these considerations, it is possible to combine the long perspective on the history of ideas with the need for a clear reading of each text against its own historical background. A text with doctrinal content can be better understood if the historian evaluating it does so with respect to the needs and conditions that existed when it was composed. It is by examining their specific contents that the texts of twelfth-century canonists or Thomas Aquinas or William of Ockham can show, for instance, how their authors used terms like *ius naturale* and *lex naturalis*. So if it is true that a specific doctrinal discourse on natural law and natural rights is the mirror of its own time, it is also true that the historical contingencies are themselves mirrored in it. The case of Ockham is significant, particularly considering the "two phases" of his discourse, which are a clear consequence of different historical contingencies. This suggests that an evaluation of the history of *ius naturale* must be carried out with consideration for the specific social, economic, political, and cultural features of each historical contingency.[6] The changes in the meaning of *ius naturale* and *lex naturalis* occurs at different moments with respect to different cultural fields. So, for instance, if the first mention of *ius naturale* in terms of "right" goes back to the mid-twelfth century, it is only since the fifteenth century that the authors of political treatises start to use the term *lex* to indicate an act of the will of a political authority. It is in fact in the rise of the modern state that legitimate law is seen as the expression of the will of the sovereign. On the contrary, the idea of *natura* as part of a metaphysical order is the subject of a crisis that starts in the thirteenth-century debates on the Aristotelian doctrines and ends only in the late sixteenth century, with the rise of the idea of nature proper to modern science.[7]

This distinctive and diachronic development of the lexicon of natural law and natural rights is characterized also by its various uses by contemporary authors. Tierney's studies on the development of conciliar theory and papal infallibility clearly show how the same lexicon, in the first decades of the fourteenth century, is used to support both perspectives.[8] Moreover, within the same framework of the Franciscan order, these lemmas and ideas were used to justify the supreme authority of the pope. With the crisis of papal authority the same notions became arguments in favor of the rediscovery of the ecclesiological principle, "quod omnes tangit ab omnibus approbari debet" (what concerns all must be approved by all).[9] So natural law and natural rights became the cornerstone of the conciliar "proposal" to reform the church.

In addition to historical contingencies, the historian must take into account the fact that the meanings of *ius naturale* and *lex naturalis* evolve and shift according to the times and places in which they were used. This is crucial for a period like the late Middle Ages, when *ius naturale* and *lex naturalis* were debated not only by theologians and exegetes but also by canonists, legists, and masters of the arts. Therefore, the historian has to evaluate the specific features of every perspective, distinguishing the legal from the theological tradition. Medieval authors saw the great works of theologians and canonists not only as the origin of specific traditions but also as the tiles in a larger mosaic, that of the human search for beatitude. Dante incisively represents this in his description of the blessed of the heaven of the Sun. In *Paradiso* 10 the poet shows the figures that symbolize Christian wisdom and associates, for instance, theologians such as Thomas Aquinas, Bonaventure, and Albert the Great with a master of the arts such as Siger of Brabant. Among these authors who glorified "theological wisdom," Dante also places Gratian, the great collector of the laws of the church, the one "who to either forum lent / Such help, as favour wins in Paradise" (*che l'uno e l'altro foro / auitò sì che piace in paradiso*).[10] Therefore, we have to investigate the historical features of medieval culture and civilization in order to understand the medieval idea of *ius naturale*, Dante's *drittura*.

# NOTES

## Preface

1. Dante Alighieri, *Tre donne*, vv. 34–36, in *Opere*, vol. 1: *Rime, Vita Nova, De Vulgari Eloquentia*, edited by Claudio Giunta, Guglielmo Gorni, and Mirko Tavoni, with introduction by Marco Santagata (Milan: Arnoldo Mondadori, 2011), 514. English translation in *Dante's Rime*, translated by Patrick S. Diehl (Princeton, NJ: Princeton University Press, 1979), 191.

2. For the interpretation of Dante's poem *Tre donne*, see the commentary of Claudio Giunta in Dante, *Opere*, 513–39. On Dante's doctrine of law, see Justin Steinberg, *Dante and the Limits of the Law* (Chicago: University of Chicago Press, 2014).

3. *The Divine Comedy of Dante Alighieri*, vol. 1: *Inferno*, edited and translated by Robert M. Durling (New York: Oxford University Press, 1996), 105.

4. Pietro Alighieri, *Super Dantis comoediam commentum*: "Quaerit si *aliquis iustus est ibi* [62]; cui respondet: *quod duo sunt justi* in mundo principaliter, scilicet, quibus genus humanum regitur, videlicet jus et mores, ut ait Gratianus in principio Decretorum, *qui ibi non audiuntur* in effectu. Vel sunt illa duo principalia jura, et neutrum ipsorum auditur: primum, scilicet fas, quod est jus divinum et naturale, per quod quisque jubetur alteri facere quod sibi vult fieri, et prohibetur alteri inferre quod fieri sibi non vult. Unde Christus in Evangelio: *quodcumque vultis faciant vobis homines, et idem facite illis*. Et hoc jus est illa dirictura, de qua auctor iste dicit in illa cantilena: *Tre donne intorno al cor* ec. Item secundum justum est jus gentium, sive jus humanum, quod vult jus suum unicuique tribuere, et neminem cum alterius jactura locupletari. Et istud jus quodammodo filius est superioris juris et patris quodammodo legis, ut in dicta cantilena dicitur. Et ista duo justa, idest jura, ibi non audiuntur in effectu, in usurpando unus alteri et odio habendo. Et hoc propter illa tria ibi potissime regnantia, de quibus sequitur." The commentary is available on the website of the Dartmouth Dante Project: http://dante.dartmouth.edu/.

5. In *Paradiso* 19.88–90, Dante notes, "Cotanto è giusto quanto a lei consuona: / nullo creato bene a sé la tira, / ma essa, radiando, lui cagiona." These verses recall the definition of *ius* found in Dante's *Monarchia* 2.2.25: "Ius in rebus nichil est aliud quam similitudo divinae voluntatis; unde fit quod quicquid divine voluntati non consonat, ipsum ius esse non possit, et quicquid divine voluntati est consonum, ius ipsum sit."

6. Harold Berman, *Law and Revolution: The Formation of the Western Legal Tradition* (Cambridge, MA: Harvard University Press, 1983); Paolo Prodi, *Una storia della giustizia: Dal pluralismo dei fori al moderno dualismo tra coscienza e diritto* (Bologna: Il Mulino, 2000).

## Introduction
### QUESTIONS AND RESEARCH

1. Several scholars, mainly those within an Anglo-Saxon and French milieu, saw in medieval debates on *ius naturale* the origin of the idea of "natural rights" that would be taken up in the constitutional documents of the American and French Revolutions. See on this, Alessandro Passerin d'Entrèves, *Natural Law: An Introduction to Legal Philosophy* (New York: Hutchinson's University Library, 1951; New Brunswick, NJ: Transaction Publishers, 1994), 51–53, 63; Brian Tierney, *The Idea of Natural Rights: Studies on Natural Rights, Natural Law, and Church Law, 1150–1625* (Atlanta, GA: Scholar Press, 1997), 1–2. Other scholars assume that the idea of natural rights marks the beginning of the modern age.

2. See Herbert L. A. Hart, "Are There Any Natural Rights?," *Philosophical Review* 64 (1955): 175–91. On Hart, see Neil MacCormick, *H. L. A. Hart* (London: Edward Arnold, 1981). The debate on natural rights and the literature it produced is presented, even if not completely, in Rex Martin and James W. Nickel, "A Bibliography of the Nature and Foundations of Rights," *Political Theory* 6 (1978): 395–413. Useful syntheses of the debate are offered in Jerome J. Shestack, "The Philosophical Foundations of Human Rights," *Human Rights Quarterly* 20 (1998): 201–34; Kenneth Cmiel, "The Recent History of Human Rights," *American Historical Review* 109 (2004): 117–35. A more general account is offered by Marcello Flores, *Storia dei diritti umani* (Bologna: Il Mulino, 2008).

3. Arthur O. Lovejoy, *The Great Chain of Being: A Study of the History of an Idea* (Cambridge, MA: Harvard University Press, 1936).

4. Lovejoy went back to the issue of the history of ideas in Arthur O. Lovejoy, "Reflections on the History of Ideas," *Journal of the History of Ideas* 1 (1940): 2–23. A clear account of the debates over Lovejoy's theory of the history of ideas is offered in Daniel J. Wilson, "Lovejoy's 'The Great Chain of Being' after Fifty Years," *Journal of the History of Ideas* 48 (1987): 187–206. See also Francis Oakley, "Lovejoy's Unexpected Option," *Journal of the History of Ideas* 48 (1987): 231–45; John Patrick Diggins, "Arthur O. Lovejoy and the Challenge of Intellectual History," *Journal of the History of Ideas* 67 (2006): 181–208.

5. See Daniele Menozzi, *Chiesa e diritti umani* (Bologna: Il Mulino, 2012), 70–80. Leo XIII offered an account of Catholic doctrine on *lex naturae* in the encyclical *Libertas* (1888). The importance of natural law in the development of neo-Thomism and neo-scholasticism is well exemplified by the famous article of Agostino Gemelli, "Medievalismo," *Vita e pensiero* 1 (1914): 1–24, reprinted in Agostino Gemelli, *Idee e battaglie per la cultura cattolica* (Milan: Società editrice "Vita e Pensiero," 1931), 3–33. Gemelli offered a more philosophical explanation of his position in Agostino Gemelli, "Leggende e pregiudizi in tema di Scolastica," *Rivista di filosofia neoscolastica* 7 (1915): 3–27. On the influence of this Catholic neo-Thomism on the juridical field, see Carlo Fantappiè, *Chiesa romana e modernità giuridica*, vol. 1: *L'edificazione del sistema canonistico (1563–1903)* (Milan: Giuffrè Editore, 2008), 199–261.

6. See Menozzi, *Chiesa e diritti umani*, 121–22. Pius XI's new emphasis on natural law as the proper foundation of a right moral and political order was also at the basis of the complex relations with the Nazi regime in Germany. See M. Patti, *Chiesa cattolica tedesca e Terzo Reich (1933–1945)* (Brescia: Morcelliana, 2008); Menozzi, *Chiesa e diritti umani*, 124–26.

7. See as significant examples, Jacques Maritain, "L'idéal historique d'une nouvelle chrétienté," in *La vie intellectuelle* (Paris: Aubin, 1935); Jacques Maritain, *Humanisme intégral: Problèmes temporels et spirituels d'une nouvelle chrétienté* (Paris: Ferdinand Aubier, 1936); Marie-Dominique Chenu, *Dimension nouvelle de la chrétienté* (Paris: Le Cerf, 1937); Marie-Dominique Chenu, "Review of Jacques Maritain, *Humanisme intégral*," *Bulletin thomiste* 15 (1938): 360–64. See Daniele Menozzi, "La chiesa e la storia: Una dimensione della cristianità da Leone XIII al Vaticano II," *Cristianesimo nella storia* 5 (1985): 69–106, esp. 86–96, for a detailed presentation of the positions of Maritain and Chenu, as well as those of the other authors involved in the debate on the new Christianity.

A more general consideration on the European consequences of scholasticism and neo-scholasticism can be found in Alan P. Fimister, *Robert Schuman: Neo-Scholastic Humanism and the Reunification of Europe* (Brussels: P. I. E. Peter Lang, 2008).

8. Martin Grabmann, "Das Naturrecht der Scholastik von Gratian bis Thomas von Aquin," *Archiv für Rechtsphilosophie* 26 (1922): 12–53, reprinted in *Mittelalterliches Geistesleben: Abhandulungen zur Geschichte der Scholastik und Mystik* (Munich: Max Huber Verlag, 1926), 65–103. Subsequent citations are to *Mittelalterliches Geistesleben*.

9. Ibid., 101–2.

10. Odon Lottin, "Le droit naturel chez saint Thomas et ses prédécesseurs," *Ephemerides theologicae Lovanienses* 1 (1924): 369–88; 2 (1925): 32–53, 345–66; 3 (1926): 155–76. These articles were published as *Le droit naturel chez saint Thomas d'Aquin et ses prédécesseurs* (Bruges: Ch. Beyaert, 1931). See also the following: "La définition classique de la loi: Commentaires historique de la Ia IIae q. 90," *Revue néo-scholastique de philosophie* 27 (1925): 129–45, 243–73, reprinted as "La loi en général: La définition thomiste et ses antécédents," in Odon Lottin, *Psychologie et morale aux XIIe et XIIIe siècles*, vol. 2: *Problèmes de morale* (Gembloux: Duculot, 1948), 9–47; "Les premiers exposés scolastiques sur la loi éternelle," *Ephemerides theologicae Lovanienses* 14 (1937): 287–301, reprinted as "La loi éternelle chex saint Thomas d'Aquin et ses prédécesseurs," in Lottin, *Psychologie et morale*, 49–67; "La loi naturelle depuis le début du XIIe siècle jusqu'à saint Thomas d'Aquin," in Lottin, *Psychologie et morale*, 69–100.

11. Lottin, "Le droit naturel," 174–76.

12. Étienne Gilson, *L'esprit de la philosophie médiévale* (Paris: Vrin, [1932] 1969). I quote from the edition of 1969.

13. Ibid., 309–10.

14. Ibid., 315–16.

15. A useful picture of the features of German legal tradition in the nineteenth century, particularly the second half, and of its influence in the evolution of canon law is offered in Alberto Melloni, "Diritto canonico," in *Dizionario del sapere storico-religioso del Novecento*, edited by Alberto Melloni (Bologna: Il Mulino, 2010), 647–53. See also the panorama offered in Carlo Fantappiè, "Diritto canonico codificato," in *Dizionario del sapere storico-religioso del Novecento*, 654–700. Both Melloni and Fantappiè provide an extensive bibliography. A useful presentation is offered in Peter Bender, *Die Rezeption des römischen Rechts im Urteil der*

*deutschen Rechtswissenschaft* (Frankfurt am Main: Peter Lang, 1979). Particularly relevant to the understanding of the German cultural framework in which several authors debated natural law is also Martin Grabmann, *Die Geschichte der katholischen Theologie seit dem Ausgang der Väterzeit* (Freiburg im Breigau: Herder, 1933), 226–48. The debate among canonists during the second half of the nineteenth century is the very background against which the scholars started their historical research on sources and documents in order to rethink the nature and development of the history of canon law. It is significant that authors such as Emil Friedberg and Johann Friedrich von Schulte, both of whom published crucial editions of medieval texts of canon law, were deeply involved in the juridical debate about the nature of canon law. A detailed presentation of this debate and its importance for the history of the church and European culture in the nineteenth and twentieth centuries is offered in Fantappié, *Chiesa romana e modernità giuridica*, vol. 2: *Il Codex iuris canonici (1917)* (Milan: Giuffrè Editore, 2008), 543–637. A careful reconstruction of the nineteenth-century debate on natural law in German Catholic culture is offered in Alexander Hollerbach, "Das Verhältnis der katholischen Naturrechtslehre des 19. Jahrhunderts zur Geschichte der Rechtswissenschaft und Rechtsphilosophie," in *Theologie und Sozialethik im Spannungsfeld der Gesellschaft: Untersuchungen zur Ideengeschichte des deutschen Katholizismus im 19. Jahrhundert*, edited by Albrecht Langner (Munich: Schöningh, 1974), 113–33.

16. On the intellectual context of Gierke's research, see Ernst Troeltsch, "The Idea of Natural Rights and Humanity," in Otto von Gierke, *Political Theories of the Middle Ages*, translated with an introduction by Frederic William Maitland (Cambridge: Cambridge University Press, 1900), 201–22, esp. 215–20. See also Angelo Bolaffi, *Il crepuscolo della sovranità: Filosofia e politica nella Germania del Novecento* (Romae Donzelli, 2002), 151–59. On Gierke and his intellectual influence, see Reinhard Höhn, *Otto von Gierke Staatslehre und unsere Zeit: Zugleich eine Auseinandersetzung mit dem Rechtssystem des 19. Jahrhunderts* (Hamburg: Hanseatische Verlagsanstalt, 1936); Hans Krupa, "Genossenschaftslehre und soziologischer Pluralismus: Ein Beitrag zur Staatslehre Otto von Gierkes," *Archiv des öffentlichen Rechts* 32 (1940–41): 97–114; Gerhard Dilcher, "Genossenschaftstheorie und Sozialrecht: Ein Juristensozialismus Otto von Gierkes?," *Quaderni fiorentini* 3–4 (1974–75): 319–65; Maximilian Fuchs, "La 'Genossenschaftstheorie' di Otto von Gierke come fonte primaria della teoria generale del diritto di Santi Romano,"

*Materiali per una storia della cultura giuridica* 9 (1979): 65–80. On the relation between Gierke's scientific work and his contemporary social and political context, see Susanne Pfeiffer-Munz, *Soziales Recht ist deutsches Recht: Otto von Gierkes Theorie des sozialen Rechts untersucht anhand seiner Stellungnahmen zur deutschen und zur schweizerischen Privatrechtskodifikation* (Zurich: Schulthess, 1979). On Gierke, see also John D. Lewis, *The Genossenschaft Theory of Otto von Gierke: A Study in Political Thought* (Madison: University of Wisconsin Press, 1935).

17. Gierke, *Political Theories of the Middle Ages.* A development of Gierke's analysis of the foundation of modern state doctrines based on natural law is offered in the fourth volume of his *Das deutsche Genossenschaftsrecht*, 4 vols. (Berlin: Weidmann, 1868–1913), which was translated into English in 1934. See Otto von Gierke, *Natural Law and the Theory of Society, 1500 to 1800, with a Lecture on the Ideas of Natural Law and Humanity by Ernst Troeltsch*, translated with an introduction by Ernest Barker (Cambridge: Cambridge University Press, 1934; Boston: Beacon Press, 1957).

18. See on this Frederic William Maitland, "Translator's Introduction," in Gierke, *Political Theories of the Middle Ages*, vii–xlvi, esp. vii–viii.

19. Gierke, *Political Theories of the Middle Ages*, 74.

20. Gierke explains his general understanding of the historical reasons that led medieval authors to define the idea of natural law as follows: "The work of development [of the medieval doctrine of Nature-Right or Natural Law] was done partly by Legists and Decretists on the ground provided by the texts of Roman and Canon Law, and partly by Divines and Philosophers on the ground of Patristic and Classical Philosophy. Thomas Aquinas drew the great outlines for the following centuries. To say more would be needless, for, however many disputes there might be touching the origin of Natural Law and the ground of its obligatory force, all were agreed that there was Natural Law, which, on the one hand, radiated from a principle transcending earthly power, and, on the other hand, was true and perfectly binding Law. Men supposed therefore that before the State existed the *Lex Naturalis* already prevailed as an obligatory statute, and that immediately or mediately from this flowed those rules of right to which the State owed even the possibility of its own rightful origin. And men also taught that the highest power on earth was subject to the rules of Natural Law. They stood above the Pope and above the Kaiser, above the Ruler and above the Sovereign People, nay, above the whole Community of Mortals. Neither statute nor act of government, neither resolution of the People nor custom could

break the bounds that thus were set. Whatever contradicted the eternal and immutable principles of Natural Law was utterly void and would bind no one." Gierke, *Political Theories of the Middle Ages*, 75.

21. Gierke, *Political Theories of the Middle Ages*, 99–100; Gierke, *Natural Law and the Theory of Society*, 35–40.

22. Robert Warraud Carlyle and Alexander James Carlyle, *A History of the Mediaeval Political Theory in the West*, vol. 5: *The Political Theory of the Thirteenth Century* (Edinburgh: William Blackwood & Sons, 1903).

23. Ibid., 36–44.

24. Ibid., 459–60.

25. John Neville Figgis, *Political Thought from Gerson to Grotius, 1414–1625* (Cambridge: Cambridge University Press, 1907). I use the Harper Torchbooks edition with an introduction by Garrett Mattingly (New York: Harper & Brothers, 1960). Figgis's basic assumption in his evaluation of medieval heritage in political thought is that in the Middle Ages there was no distinction between church and state for the church was the state. See Garrett Mattingly, "Introduction to the Torchbook Edition," in Figgis, *Political Thought*, ix–xxii, esp. xii. Precisely this circumstance can explain why political theories and ideas such as natural law as the limit to the exercise of an absolute political power were developed inside the framework of the religious culture of medieval civilization. It is only with Machiavelli, Figgis notes, that political theory became independent from theology. Figgis, *Political Thought*, 20–22. For what concerns Figgis's evaluation of the historical reconstruction of Carlyle and Carlyle, see his reviews of volumes 1–3 of *A History of Medieval Political Theory in the West*, in *English Historical Review* 19.74 (1904): 330–33; 25.99 (1910): 561–64; 31.122 (1916): 305–6, respectively.

26. Figgis, *Political Thought*, 8.

27. Ibid., 9: "It was Lord Acton who said that 'not the devil but S. Thomas Aquinas was the first Whig.' With the revived study of Roman Law there had come an increasing reverence for the Natural Law with which even a Pope cannot dispense. This notion was to be of great service to all theorists, who desired to subject to some limits the all-embracing activity of the modern state, whether these limits were internal and concerned the interests of individuals or external and imposed on the ground of international equity."

28. Ibid.

29. See in particular Hans Kelsen, *General Theory of Law and State* (Cambridge, MA: Harvard University Press, 1945).

30. See on this Hans Kelsen, "The Natural-Law Doctrine before the Tribunal of Science," *Western Political Quarterly* 2.4 (1949): 481–513. See Edgar Bodenheimer's response: "The Natural-Law Doctrine before the Tribunal of Science: A Reply to Hans Kelsen," *Western Political Quarterly* 3.3 (1950): 335–63.

31. World War II marks a crisis in the development of legal and political doctrines. Several European thinkers who left Germany and Europe between the 1930s and the 1940s devoted their attention to a reconsideration of the natural law theories as an intellectual weapon against totalitarianism. In particular, several authors stressed the need to look back to the medieval roots of this theory as a means to establish effective limits to the exercise of absolute power. See on this Heinrich Rommen, *Die ewige Wiederkehr des Naturrechts* (Leipzig: Jakob Hegner, 1936); the English edition of this book appeared as *The Natural Law: A Study in Legal and Social History and Philosophy*, translated by Thomas R. Hanley (Washington, DC: Herder, 1947), second edition edited by Russel Hittinger (Indianapolis: Liberty Fund, 1998); Yves R. Simon, *Philosophy of Democratic Government* (Chicago: University of Chicago Press, 1951); Jacques Maritain, *Man and the State* (Washington, DC: Catholic University of America Press, 1951); Eric Voegelin, *The New Science of Politics* (Chicago: University of Chicago Press, 1952); Leo Strauss, *Natural Rights and History: A Cogent Examination of one of the Most Significant Issues in Modern Political and Social Philosophy* (Chicago: University of Chicago Press, 1953). This kind of political discourse on natural law in the cultural context of the United States contributed to a reconsideration of the possible links between American constitutionalism and the Catholic idea of natural law. See on this John Courtney Murray, *We Hold These Truths: Catholic Reflections on the American Proposition* (Kansas City: Sheed & Ward, 1960).

32. Passerin d'Entrèves, *Natural Law*. This volume is the result of a series of lectures that the author gave in 1948 at the University of Chicago.

33. Passerin d'Entrèves explains the features of his study of natural law in a passage that is useful to quote: "I think that this is, on the whole, a much more satisfactory approach to the problem of natural law than the purely historical one. For one thing it accounts for the fact that there is really not one tradition of natural law, but many. The medieval and the modern conceptions of natural law are two different doctrines; the continuity between them is mainly a question of words. The philosophical approach also allows for the grouping of different authors on deeper than mere chronological grounds. If Cicero and Locke agree in their definition

of natural law, this is an indication of a more intimate link than mere imitation or repetition. Finally, only philosophy can provide the clue to the problems which history lays bare but is unable to solve. If the modern doctrine of natural law proved to be so different from the old both in its implications and in its after-reaching consequence, the reason is that a new conception of man and universe turned what had been for centuries a harmless and orthodox doctrine into a potent instrument of progress and revolution, which gave an entirely new turn to history and of which we still feel the effects." Passerin d'Entrèves, *Natural Law*, 17. Cary Nederman efficaciously describes Passerin d'Entrèves's method of studying natural law as a combination of "historical narrative and philosophical inquiry." Cary Nedermann, "Introduction to the Transaction Edition," in Passerin d'Entrèves, *Natural Law*, xiv.

34. On the Roman idea of natural law, see Passerin d'Entrèves, *Natural Law*, 22–35, esp. 35; for medieval doctrines, see 37–50.

35. Passerin d'Entrèves, *Natural Law*, 49.

36. Ibid., 51–64, esp. 61–62.

37. Ibid., 78.

38. Ibid., 91.

39. Ibid., 105–7.

40. Explaining the contribution of medieval canonists and theologians to the development of a new system of natural law, with respect to ancient Roman culture, Passerin d'Entrèves notes: "The lawyers of the Church—the Canonists—stand out among medieval lawyers for the freedom and daring with which they recast the whole problem of law and morals. They gave natural law an unprecedented coherence, clearness and force. Canon law has been said, and correctly, to constitute the principal vehicle, in the Middle Ages, of the doctrine of the law of nature." Passerin d'Entrèves, *Natural Law*, 37–38. The Italian scholar devoted other writings to the analysis of medieval political thought and its acquisition. See Alessandro Passerin d'Entrèves, *La filosofia politica medioevale: Appunti di storia delle dottrine politiche* (Turin: Giappichelli, 1934); and *Medieval Contribution to Political Thought: Thomas Aquinas, Marsilius of Padua, Richard Hooker* (New York: Humanities Press, 1959).

41. See in particular Otto Brunner, Werner Conze, and Reinhart Koselleck, eds., *Geschichtliche Grundbegriffe: Historisches Lexikon zur politisch-sozialen Sprache in Deutschland* (Stuttgart: Klett-Cotta, 1972–97); Reinhart Koselleck, "Historik und Hermeneutik," in Reinhart Koselleck, *Kritik und Krise: Ein Beitrag zur Pathogenese der bürgerlichen*

*Welt* (Freiburg: K. Alber, 1959); Reinhart Koselleck, *Zeitschichten: Studien zur Historik. Mit einem Beitrag von Hans-Georg Gadamer* (Frankfurt am Main: Suhrkamp Verlag, 2000), 97–127. For a general presentation of the German *Begriffsgeschichte*, see Merio Scattola, "Storia dei concetti e storia delle discipline politiche," *Storia della storiografia* 49 (2006), 95–124; Diego Fusaro, *L'orizzonte in movimento: Modernità e futuro in Reinhardt Koselleck* (Bologna: Il Mulino, 2012).

42. See Scattola, "Storia dei concetti e storia delle discipline," 108–9. A significant example of the understanding of the notion of natural law according to the *Begriffsgeschichte* is offered in Karl-Heinz Ilting, "Naturrecht," in *Geschichtliche Grundbegriffe*, 4:245–313.

## Chapter 1
### OBJECTIVITY VERSUS SUBJECTIVITY

1. See in particular Michel Villey's *Précis de philosophie du droit*, 2 vols. (Paris: Dalloz, 1977–78); *Le droit et les droits de l'homme* (Paris: Presses Universitaires de France, 1983); *Seize essais de philosophie du Droit dont un sur la crise universitaire* (Paris: Dalloz, 1969); and *Cours d'histoire de la philosophie du droit* (Paris: Dalloz, 1962). On Villey's position on natural rights, see Jean-Pierre Schouppe, "Reflexions sur la conception du droit de M. Villey: une alternative à son rejet des droits de l'homme," *Persona y derecho* 25 (1991): 151–69; Gregorio Peces-Barba Martinez, "Michel Villey et les droits de l'homme," *Droit et société* 71 (2009): 93–100.

2. See Michel Villey, *Leçons d'histoire de la philosophie du droit* (Paris: Dalloz, 1957), 337–47.

3. A passage in the conclusions of Tierney's study devoted to the origins of papal infallibility exemplifies quite well his perspective. Here Tierney explains how he considers his own scientific perspective as a historian with respect to that of a theologian. He notes that the theologian needs to look at history to have some kind of understanding of the "development" and thus of the "changes" that occurred in the history of the church. He writes, "All definitions of Christian faith are expressions of the life of the church as it existed at some particular time and place. (We do not detract from the unique authority of Scripture when we acknowledge that this is true also of the Gospels.) The expression of Christian truth through the necessary medium of the changing human cultures that have succeeded one another in time gives rise to possibilities of error, as we

have observed. But it is precisely this historical process—if the theologian will make himself aware of it—that also makes possible a deepening understanding of the truth. Every Christian civilization will make its own errors; but also, characteristically, its particular emphases will illuminate new facets of divine truth. Each fresh generation succeeds to a richer heritage of Christian insights, perceptions, intuitions, which it can use—if it so chooses—to inform its own understanding of the faith. It also acquires a new perspective from which to judge what is ephemeral in the church's attempts to explicate its faith and what is enduring. (To many contemporary Catholics it seems that the various nineteenth-century papal pronouncements condemning the principle of religious toleration can be dismissed as ephemeral products of a particular historical situation; at the time of their promulgation they were widely accepted as enduring statements of Catholic truth.) It is good then for a scholar who would expound the faith of the church to know something of the church's history. Any meaningful theory of development of doctrine must be based on a consideration of the whole experience of the church in time." Brian Tierney, *Origins of Papal Infallibility, 1150–1350: A Study on the Concepts of Infallibility, Sovereignty and Tradition in the Middle Ages*, Second Impression with a postscript (Leiden: Brill, 1988), 278–79.

4. See Michel Villey, "L'idée du droit subjectif et les systèmes juridiques romains," *Revue historique de droit française et étranger* 24 (1946): 207–21; "Les origines de la notion de droit subjectif," *Archives de philosophie du droit* 2 (1953–54): 163–87; and "Suum jus cuique tribuere," in *Studi in onore di Pietro de Francisci*, 4 vols. (Milan: Giuffrè Editore, 1956), 1:361–71.

5. See Michel Villey, "Le 'jus in re' du droit romain classique au droit moderne," "L'idée du droit subjectif," and "Suum jus cuique tribuere," all in Michel Villey, *Conférence faites à l'Institut de Droit Romain en 1947* (Paris: Institut de Droit Romain, 1950), 187–225, 217, 364, respectively.

6. See in particular Martin Grabmann, "Das Naturrecht der Scholastik von Gratian bis Thomas von Aquin," *Archiv für Rechtsphilosophie* 26 (1922): 12–53, reprinted in *Mittelalterliches Geistesleben: Abhandlungen zur Geschichte der Scholastik und Mystik*, 65–103 (Munich: Max Huber Verlag, 1926); Odon Lottin, *Le droit naturel chez Saint Thomas d'Aquin et ses prédécesseurs* (Bruges: Ch. Beyaert, 1931).

7. Michel Villey, *La formation de la pensée juridique moderne: Cours d'histoire de la philosophie du droit* (Paris: Edition Montchretien, 1975), 12–13: "Au Moyen Âge, la culture est entre les mains des théologiens:

écoles religieuses du XII^{ème} siècle (Chartres–Laon–Paris) Universités des XII^{ème} et XIII^{ème} siècles. Peu de philosophie du droit aussi célèbres, aussi notables que celle incluse dans la *Somme théologique* de saint Thomas. Peu d'événements aussi chargés de conséquences que l'avénement de la scolastique franciscaine (Scott, Guillaume d'Occam). Mais, ce qui est plus méconnu, l'époque moderne a conservé, bien que la culture y soit passée largement au mond des laïcs (la distinction de clercs et laïcs ayant perdu son sens chez les protestants), des préoccupations religieuses et théologiques. Le XVI^{ème} siècle n'est pas incroyant (Lucien Febvre: *Rabelais et le pro-blème de l'incroyance au XVI^{ème} siècle*), et la philosophie du droit y est représentée d'abord par les théologiens espagnols de la Réforme catholique (Vitoria–Suárez–F. Vazquez). Luther, Calvin, les calvinistes approtent une pensée sur le droit. Grotius, Puffendorf, Locke, Spinoza, Leibniz, Wolf et Kant ont tuos écrit des ouvrages de théologie, qui, en leur temps, ne furent pas les moins célèbres de leurs oeuvres. Seuls les 'philosophes' français du XVIII^{ème} siècle commencent à faire exception, encore qu'ils ne soient pas exempts, de façon négative, de préoccupations religieuses. Il est donc conforme à la verité historique de restituer aux doctrines de ces anciens auteurs sur le droit cette *dimension religieuse* qui leur était essentielle. Mais on notera pour terminer que 'la philosophie du droit chez les théologiens du Christianisme,' etant donné le rôle éminent de la raison profane dans leur oeuvre, c'est à peu de chose près toute l'histoire de la philosophie du droit de l'Europe jusqu'au XVIII^{ème} siècle." See also Villey, *La formation*, 109, where he quotes A. Forest, F. Van Steenberghen, and M. de Gandil-lac, in *Histoire de l'Église*, vol. 13: *Le mouvement doctrinal du XIème au XIVème siècle* (Paris: Bloud & Gay, 1956); Jacques Chevalier, *Histoire de la pensée*, vol. 2: *La pensée chrétienne* (Paris: Flammarion, 1956); Marie-Dominique Chenu, *La théologie comme science au XIIIème siècle* (Paris: Vrin, 1957); Philippe Delhaye, *La philosophie chrétienne au Moyen Âge* (Paris: Fayard, 1959); Étienne Gilson, *La philosophie au Moyen Âge* (Paris: Payot, 1962).

8. Villey shares with Gilson the idea that Augustine's writings con-stitute the basis for a Christian understanding of *ius* and *lex*. See Villey, *Leçons d'histoire*, 41–42; Villey, *La formation*, 73–74 ; and Étienne Gilson, *Introduction à l'étude de Saint Augustin* (Paris: Vrin, 1927).

9. Villey, *Leçons d'histoire*, 42: "Le problème de l'influence de la pensée chrétienne sur la tradition juridique ne peut être traité qu'à l'aide d'une distinction chronologique. Nous distinguerons deux périodes: De la

conversion de Constantin jusqu'au XIII<sup>e</sup> siècle: un droit chrétien se constitue. Du début du XIV<sup>e</sup> siècle jusqu'à nos jours, s'opère la laïcisation du droit."

10. See Villey, *Leçons d'histoire*, 44–45; Villey, *La formation*, 74–78.

11. Villey, *Leçons d'histoire*, 46. Villey summarizes the main features of the Augustinian heritage in the Middle Ages, stressing Augustine's importance for later thirteenth-century developments. Villey, *La formation*, 104: "Droit qui est morale, et morale de charité. A cela conduit saint Augustin. L'entreprise n'a rien d'impossible de fonder un ordre social aussi bien sur la rectitude des dispositions morales que sur la justice objective, mathématisante d'Aristote. Et l'usage étant le seul maître du sens des mots, au regard de l'historien, c'est cet effort de concordance à la loi divine, reconnu par l'élite dirigeante pour vraie norme de vie sociale, que signifia, dans cette société, le mot *droit.*"

12. Villey, *La formation*, 108: "Conquis très tôt après Gratien à la nouvelle science, les décrétistes juxtaposent, confrontant, s'efforcent de concilier à la définition sacrale canonique du droit naturel, le texte d'Ulpien, ou celui de Paul, ou souvent ceux de Cicéron. Et des doutes naissent sur l'origine sacrale du droit, sur l'aptitude des préceptes évangeliques à servir de préceptes de droit devant des tribunaux terrestres."

13. Ibid., 115: "La notion de *nature* revient à l'ordre du jour. Alain de Lille lui consacre un grand poème allégorique (*De planctu naturae*), fait l'apologie du mariage comme conforme aux fins de la nature (la propagation de l'espèce), attaque les vices « contre nature » contraires à ces mêmes fins. Et voici restaurées les bases de la philosophie classique du droit naturel. Alimenté par la lecture du *Timée* de Platon, d'oeuvres néoplatoniciennes, le thème se répand que Dieu agit par de « *causes secondes* » ; qu'en même temps qu'il créa le monde il l'a soumis à des lois fixes, à l'ordre immuable d'une nature, ce qui est aussi la condition d'une renaissance des sciences physiques (cf. les études de Ph. Delhaye). On aurait probablement tort de trop s'attarder sur des œuvres encore hésitantes et sans doute mineures, comparées aux chef-d'œuvre de saint Thomas; mais quand nous verrons saint Thomas doter les juristes d'une doctrine du droit, adaptée aux besoins pratiques de leur temps, et contrastant fortement de l'augustinisme, n'oublions pas que la nouveauté apparente de sa doctrine est sortie d'une siècle et demi d'efforts, de travaux, de combats pour faire revivre le meilleur de la philosophie antique."

14. See Villey, *Leçons d'histoire*, 49.

15. Villey, *La formation*, 126–27: "Au delà des faites les *natures*. Et c'est ici que le travail de l'intelligence (selon cette philosophie classique du droit naturel) mène à la connaissance du droit. Car, puisque l'ordre est dans la nature, c'est l'ordre que la science saisit avec la nature, le désordre qu'elle élimine. Noter intellect, subdivisé en « speculatif » et « pratique » ne constitute dans ces deux fonctions qu'une seule et unique « puissance » (Ia, q. 79, art. 11) et savoir l'*essence* d'une chose serait déjà connaître sa *fin*. L'*être* d'une chose que poursuit l'intelligence spéculative, est son devoir-être, son bien. '*Mens et bonum convertuntur.*' L'essence de l'homme, quant à son corps, ce n'est pas l'homme brogne, ni le boiteux, ni le dégénéré: plutôt l'homme du canon grec."

16. S. Thomae de Aquino, *Summa theologiae*, Ia, q. 87, art. 1: "Non . . . per essentiam suam, sed per actum suum se cognoscit intellectus noster. Et hoc dupliciter. Uno quidem modo, particulariter, secundum quod Socrates vel Plato percipit se habere animam intellectivam, ex hoc quod percipit se intelligere. Alio modo, in universali, secundum quod naturam humanae mentis ex actu intellectus consideramus. Sed verum est quod iudicium et efficacia huius cognitionis per quam naturam animae cognoscimus, competit nobis secundum derivationem luminis intellectus nostri a veritate divina, in qua rationes omnium rerum continentur, sicut supra dictum est. Unde et Augustinus dicit, in IX de Trin., *intuemur inviolabilem veritatem, ex qua perfecte, quantum possumus, definimus non qualis sit uniuscuiusque hominis mens, sed qualis esse sempiternis rationibus debeat.* Est autem differentia inter has duas cognitiones. Nam ad primam cognitionem de mente habendam, sufficit ipsa mentis praesentia, quae est principium actus ex quo mens percipit seipsam. Et ideo dicitur se cognoscere per suam praesentiam. Sed ad secundam cognitionem de mente habendam, non sufficit eius praesentia, sed requiritur diligens et subtilis inquisitio. Unde et multi naturam animae ignorant, et multi etiam circa naturam animae erraverunt. Propter quod Augustinus dicit, X de Trin., de tali inquisitione mentis, *non velut absentem se quaerat mens cernere; sed praesentem quaerat discernere*, idest cognoscere differentiam suam ab aliis rebus, quod est cognoscere quidditatem et naturam suam." See also Villey, *La formation*, 129–30.

17. S. Thomae de Aquino, *Summa theologiae*, Ia–IIae, q. 90, art. 3: "Lex proprie primo, et principaliter respicit ordinem ad bonum commune: ordinare autem aliquid in bonum commune, est vel totius multitudinis, vel alicuius gerentis vicem totius multitudinis: et ideo condere legem vel pertinet ad totam multitudinem, vel pertinet ad personam publicam, quae

totius multitudinis curam habet: quia et in omnibus aliis ordinare in finem est eius, cuius est proprius ille finis." See Villey, *La formation*, 131–32.

18. See Villey, *La formation*, 129–30.

19. Ibid., 174–75: "Avec le soutien apporté à la Renaissance du droit romain, sans doute est-ce là, dans son temps, le principal effet de la doctrine de saint Thomas. Le droit canonique, tenant encore le rôle majeur au XIII^ème siècle, en a le premier bénéficié. La philosophie de saint Thomas justifia dans le droit canon l'essor croissant des *Décrétales*. Les Décrétales après lui se présenteront, non plus seulement sous l'apparence d'acte judiciaires et d'interprétations d'un droit censé permanent, mais désormais comme créatrices d'un droit *nouveau* réadapté aux circonstances de l'histoire, ainsi que le veut la doctrine classique du droit naturel. . . . Mais, bien que le pape puisse prétendre à l'autorité dans cette société qu'est l'Eglise, la leçon de saint Thomas s'adresse davantage aux communautés politiques *laïques*. C'est elles qu'elle libère, et provoque chez elles l'épanouissement du droit. Dans les villes et dans les royaumes, et pour commencer dans l'empire, la seconde moitié du XIII^ème et de quatorzième siècle verront la multiplication des status et des *ordonnances*: essor d'un droit laïc armé de règles fixes et précises, qui va de pair avec le développement de l'organisation judiciaire. La philosophie de saint Thomas a parfaitement répondu aux besoins et aux possibilités des Etats modernes naissants." See also Michel Villey, "La théologie de Thomas d'Aquin et la formation de l'État moderne," in *Théologie et droit dans la science politique de l'État moderne: Actes de la table ronde de Rome (12–14 novembre 1987)* (Rome: École française de Rome, 1991), 31–49.

20. See Villey, *Leçons d'histoire*, 51–54; Villey, *La formation*, 176.

21. Georges de Lagarde, *La naissance de l'esprit laïque au déclin du Moyen Âge*, vol. 6: *L'individualisme Ockhamiste: La morale et le droit* (Paris: Presses Universitaires de France, 1946), 162–63: "Nous voyons en définitive une conception nominaliste du droit et même de la justice se substituer à la conception réaliste d'un saint Thomas. Saint Thomas avait établi une continuité entre les lois métaphysiques de l'Etre et les lois morales. Ockham nie cette continuité. La loi morale se surajoute à l'existant comme un donné arbitraire. Saint Thomas avait établi une continuité entre les préceptes de la droite raison et l'ordre de la nature conçu comme un équilibre objectif des natures et une subordination exacte de chaque être à sa fin. Ockham rompt ce lien. Les préceptes et prescriptions rationnelles qui constituent la morale sont un donné de la raison humaine et non l'expression par elle d'un équilibre qui lui soit extérieur. Saint Thomas

avait montré que la morale et le droit ne sont que les deux aspects d'un même équilibre fondamental. Ockham s'est efforcé au contraire de montrer qu'il n'y a pas nécessairement concordance entre les deux notions. . . . Nous avions déjà vu que Dieu échappait totalement à la catégorie de moralité. Nous constatons maintenant que toute une frange immense de la vie humaine, et notamment la plupart des institutions juridiques et sociales positives ne sont pas justiciables de cette catégorie, ou ne le sont qu'indirectement. Nous n'avons pas besoin d'enfler les mots pour faire percevoir l'immense révolution que cette conclusion entraîne dans la philosophie morale et sociale."

22. See de Lagarde, *La naissance de l'esprit laïque au déclin du Moyen Âge*, 6:156–58; Villey, *La formation*, 205.

23. See Villey, *La formation*, 180–81. On the issue of *potentia Dei absoluta*, see Eugenio Randi, *Il sovrano e l'orologio: Due immagini di Dio nel dibatitto sulla «potentia absoluta» fra XIII e XIV secolo* (Florence: La Nuova Italia, 1987).

24. Villey, *La formation*, 209–10: "De même qu'il suscite une crise au sein de la théologie, et qu'à long terme il renouvelle les méthodes des sciences, le nominalisme devait encore envahir le *droit*. Il y signifie l'abandon du droit naturel, c'est-à-dire de cette méthode qui avait présidé, selon nous, à la constitution de la science juridique romaine et que la scolastique humaniste venait précisément de restaurer dans le droit savant du Moyen-Âge; et qui prenait pour point de départ pour le découverte des solutions juridiques l'observation de la *Nature* et de l'ordre qu'elle recèle. Le nominalisme au contraire habitue à penser toutes choses à partir de *l'individu*. L'individu (non plus le rapport entre plusieurs individus) devient le centre d'intérêt de la science du droit; l'effort de la science juridique va désormais tendre à décrire les qualités juridiques de l'individu, l'étendue de ses facultés, de ses *droits individuels*. Et quant aux normes juridiques, faute désormais de les extraire de l'ordre même qu'auparavant on croyait lire dans la Nature, force sera d'en chercher l'origine exclusivement dans les volontés positives des individus: le *positivisme* juridique est l'enfant du nominalisme. Tous le caractères essentiels de la pensée juridique moderne sont déjà contenus en puissance dans le nominalisme."

25. Villey, *La formation*, 216.

26. Ibid., 230: "Le propre du langage juridique classique est de viser un monde de *choses*, de biens extérieurs, parce que c'est seulement dans les choses et le partage fait dans les choses que se manifeste le rapport juridique *entre* les personnes. La science du droit a les yeux tournés vers

les *choses* et c'est en quoi l'authentique langage est essentiellement *objectif*. Autre est le langage de l'individualisme. Au lieu de viser l'ordre du groupe, il est centré sur le *sujet* en particulier. Il tend à concevoir et à exprimer les «qualités» ou les «facultés» d'un sujet, les forces que son être irradie: pouvoirs, mais au sens principal du mot, comme capacité de la personne, attenant au sujet, *subjectif*. Conséquence: on conçoit ce pouvoir au départ comme *illimité*."

## Chapter 2
### THE FOUNDATION OF POLITICAL AND MORAL ORDER

1. See John Neville Figgis, *Political Thought from Gerson to Grotius, 1414–1625: Seven Studies* (Cambridge: Cambridge University Press, 1907; New York: Harper & Brothers, 1960).

2. Ibid., 41; and Francis Oakley, "Figgis, Constance, and the Divines of Paris," *American Historical Review* 75 (1969): 368–86, 369.

3. See Brian Tierney, *Foundations of the Conciliar Theory: The Contribution of the Medieval Canonists from Gratian to the Great Schism* (Cambridge: Cambridge University Press, 1955; reprint Leiden: Brill, 1998).

4. See Francis Oakley, *The Political Thought of Pierre d'Ailly: The Voluntarist Tradition* (New Haven, CT: Yale University Press, 1964), 15–16. On d'Ailly, see also Francis Oakley, "Gerson and d'Ailly: An Admonition," *Speculum* 40 (1965): 74–83, reprinted in Francis Oakley, *Natural Law, Conciliarism and Consent in the Late Middle Ages* (London: Variorum, 1984), V; Francis Oakley, "Pierre d'Ailly and the Absolute Power of God: Another Note on the Theology of Nominalism," *Harvard Theological Review* 56 (1963): 59–73, reprinted in Oakley, *Natural Law, Conciliarism and Consent*, III; Francis Oakley, "Pierre d'Ailly," in *Reformers in Profile*, ed. B. A. Gerrish (Philadelphia: Fortress Press, 1967), 40–57, reprinted in Oakley, *Natural Law, Conciliarism and Consent*, II.

5. See Francis Oakley, "Medieval Theories of Natural Law: William of Ockham and the Significance of the Voluntarist Tradition," *Natural Law Forum* 6 (1961): 65–83, reprinted in Oakley, *Natural Law, Conciliarism and Consent*, XV.

6. Gordon Leff, *Medieval Thought from St. Augustine to Ockham* (Harmondsworth: Middlesex, 1958), 258. Leff explains quite clearly how the first decades of the fourteenth century mark the rise of a new

philosophical sensibility. Leff, *Medieval Thought*, 258–59: "The atmos-
phere of fourteenth-century thought catches these changes: much of the
self-confidence in the powers of reason has evaporated by the second and
third decades. There is a similar differentiation between faith and natural knowledge to that developing between secular and spiritual authority;
there is a growing distrust of an ordered hierarchy between the tenets of
revelation and rational demonstration, at a time of mounting discontent
with a fixed social order. The union between understanding and belief is
under attack, together with much else in Christendom. There are three
dominating traits in the thought of the fourteenth century. The first is the
desire to disengage faith from reason. The revulsion against determinism
that marked the 1277 condemnations gradually spread to the attempt to
trace God from His creatures. . . . Duns Scotus was to establish this view,
which was given new application by Ockham and his followers. It made
for a redefinition of what could be known about God. The distinction
between faith and reason, to which St. Thomas had so firmly held, was
taken to make each self-contained; the natural and supernatural were not
merely on different planes but without a meeting-point; since they dealt
with different truths they could not inform one another. This led to the
second trait: the growth of rival outlooks founded upon either faith or
reason. On one side, there was an attitude which, as developed by Ockham, can best be described as empiricism; fact became the touchstone; and
to move beyond its boundaries was to enter the realm of speculation and
leave certainty. Matters of belief, and God Himself, could not be a subject
for reason, but for faith alone. To discuss them was to conjure up possibilities, not to assert the truth. . . . On the other side, faith took on an
increasingly independent attitude. It looked to revelation and authority
for its support, rather than to ratiocination. This was the other side of the
coin: if reason, the one must be as independent as the other. . . . The third
trait was a marked change in the lines of thought. It is usually common to
regard the fourteenth century as the period of the second struggle between
realism and nominalism, with Duns Scotus and William of Ockham as the
leading actors. Consequently, there has been a misleading habit of equat-
ing Scotism with realism and Ockhamism with nominalism and making
their opposition govern the intellectual history of the period. Yet the more
this view is examined, the more untenable it becomes." See also Oakley,
*Pierre d'Ailly*, 16–19, where he clearly assumes Leff's perspective as the
proper picture of the fourteenth-century philosophical panorama.

7. Oakley, "Figgis, Constance, and the Divines of Paris," 383: "All these conciliarists, to a greater or lesser degree, are theologians of nominalist sympathies. As a result, all are extremely careful to avoid implying that the freedom of the Divine Will is in any way bound either by the norms of natural morality or by the divinely established arrangements of ecclesiastical life." Oakley also suggests this historical perspective in Francis Oakley, "Natural Law, the Corpus Mysticum, and Consent in Conciliar Thought from John of Paris to Matthias Ugonis," *Speculum* 56 (1981): 786–810. See also the introduction to Francis Oakley, *Politics and Eternity: Studies in the History of Medieval and Early-Modern Political Thought* (Leiden: Brill, 1999), 1–24.

8. Oakley, *Pierre d'Ailly*, 21.

9. Ibid., 17: "The condemnations, which denounced as contrary to the Christian faith a host of philosophical propositions, several of which were Thomistic, were promulgated by Étienne Tampier, Bishop of Paris, and Robert Kilwardby, Archbishop of Canterbury. In so acting they reflected a fear, already widespread among theologians, that the metaphysical necessitarianism of Aristotle and his modern commentators, Avicenna and Averroës, endangered the Christian doctrine of the freedom and omnipotence of God. The doctrinal act of 1277, as Gilson points out, traced the condemned errors to their very root, 'namely, the Aristotelian identification of reality, intelligibility and necessity, not only in things, but first and above all in God.' The honeymoon of philosophy and theology was over, and this marked the beginning of the theological reaction that was to vindicate the freedom and omnipotence of God at the expense of the ultimate intelligibility of the world." Oakley reaffirms the importance of the 1277 condemnation in his "Pierre d'Ailly and the Absolute Power of God," 63–64. Here he agrees with Étienne Gilson's opinion that William of Ockham's thought could be considered "a post-1277 theology."

10. See Oakley, "Medieval Theories of Natural Law," 71–72.

11. Ibid., 72: "The history of the voluntarist interpretation of natural law has yet to be written, and it forms something of a subterranean stream in medieval and modern thought. This much, however, is apparent: that having been formulated with clarity by Ockham, it was propagated by his philosophical descendants, the nominalist philosophers who became so prominent in the later Middle Ages."

12. Oakley, *Pierre d'Ailly*, 171: "What Ockham did was to ground the natural law, and indeed all ethical values, on the will of God. Natural laws

ceased, therefore, to be a 'dictate of reason as to what is right, grounded in the being of God but unalterable even by Him,' and became 'a divine command . . . right and binding merely because God was the lawgiver.'"

13. Oakley, "Figgis, Constance, and the Divines of Paris," 384: "For these conciliarists, therefore, the Pauline dictum that all power is of God takes on a heightened significance. If the establishment of secular political authority, unlike ecclesiastical, is the outcome of human agencies working in accordance with the dictates of the natural law, this must not be taken to imply that that law or those agencies are autonomous. For God, after all, is 'the founder of nature,' and it is His obligating Will that establishes the natural law."

14. See Oakley, *Pierre d'Ailly*, 189–90.

15. Ibid., 191.

16. See Oakley, "Natural Law, the Corpus Mysticum, and Consent," 795–98.

17. Oakley, "Figgis, Constance, and the Divines of Paris," 386: "Such rights, after all, were rooted merely in custom or in the positive law. In going one step further and grounding them in the natural law itself, these conciliarists, then, are doing nothing less than taking the doctrine of consent that is basic to so much of medieval legal and constitutional theory and practice, disengaging it from the particularizing elements of regional, national, or ecclesiastical custom, and raising it to the level of a political philosophy."

18. See Isaiah Berlin, "Two Concepts of Liberty," in Isaiah Berlin, *Four Essays on Liberty* (Oxford: Oxford University Press, 1969); Michel Bastit, *Naissance de la loi moderne* (Paris: Presses Universitaires de France, 1990).

19. See Richard Tuck, *Natural Rights Theories: Their Origin and Development* (Cambridge: Cambridge University Press, 1979), 5. On the figure of Silvestro Mazzolini da Prierio, see Simona Feci, "Mazzolini Silvestro (Silvestro da Prierio, Prierias, Prieriate)," in *Dizionario Biografico degli Italiani*, vol. 72 (Rome: Istituto dell'Enciclopedia Italiana, 2009), 678–81.

20. Tuck, *Natural Rights Theory*.

21. Ibid., 7: "The issues at stake in the debate which Mazzolini summarised were thus the crucial ones for any understanding of the concept of a right, and the great seventeenth-century rights theories depended on its outcome."

22. Ibid., 8–9.

23. Ibid., 13: "It is among the men who rediscovered the Digest and created the medieval science of Roman law in the twelfth century that we must look to find the first modern rights theory, one built round the notion of a passive right. Their problem was to balance the legal language of their own time, derived from the vulgar law of the late Empire and the Germanic kingdoms, with what they found in the Digest, and in a sense the history of Roman law studies in the middle ages is the history of how the lawyers moved between these two poles. There is one feature which remained constant throughout the period, however, and which to some extent serves to mark medieval law studies off from those of the Renaissance: the medieval lawyer always regarded *dominium* as a *ius*, and hence was prepared to talk about *property* rights. He was not prepared to read the Digest in the counter-intuitive way practised by the Renaissance lawyer, nor to let it lead him to a fundamental modification of his existing legal concepts. As Irnerius, the founder of the law school at Bologna at the turn of the eleventh and twelfth centuries, said, '*dominium* is a kind of *ius*', and that remained a basic assumption until the Renaissance."

24. Ibid., 14.

25. Ibid., 15: "The theory of the early glossators was a formidable and plausible one. All rights were claim rights: they all required other men to act in some way towards the claimant, to grant him something. Distinctions between rights could be given by distinguishing either between the people they were claims on, or between what was being claimed; and true property, *dominium*, was defined as a claim to total control against all the world. In other words, they had evolved a consistent theory of passive rights. To a large extent, this must be bound up with the increasing sophistication and elaboration of *canon* law. It was the canon lawyers who developed and applied such important maxims as the principle that 'personal *ius*' [i.e., *iura ad rem*] cannot be transferred to others nor be the subject of contracts which picked out the central difference between the two categories. Ecclesiastical law was of course greatly concerned with general questions of welfare: in the Church, Europe had an institution unprecedented in the Roman world in that it was actually designed (at least in part) for charitable purposes. It is not surprising that a theory about rights as claims should have evolved from within an institution which was so concerned with the claims made on other men by the needy or deserving."

26. Ibid., 16.

27. Ibid.: "The recognition of the category of *dominium utile* was to transform rights theories. For now *dominium* was taken to be any *ius in re*:

*any* right which could be defended against all other men, and which could be transferred or alienated by its possessor, was a *property* right, and not only rights of total control. The process had begun whereby all of a man's rights, of whatever kind, were to come to be seen as his property. This obscure thirteenth-century feud had these tremendous consequences: there is a direct line linking Accursius with the late medieval rights theorists, and through them with the great seventeenth-century figures."

28. Ibid., 18–19.

29. S. Thomas de Aquino, *Summa theologiae* Ia–IIae, q. 94, a. 5: "Aliquid dicitur esse de iure naturali dupliciter: uno modo, quia ad hoc natura inclinat, siciut non esse iniuriam, alteri faciendam; alio modo, quia natura non inducit contrariam, sicut possemus dicere quod hominem esse nudum est de iure naturali, quia natura non dedit ei vestitum, sed ars adinvenit. Et hoc modo communis omnium possessio et una libertas dicitur esse de iure naturali, quia scilicet distinctio possessionum et servitus non sunt inductae a natura, sed per hominum rationem ad utilitatem humanae vitae." See Tuck, *Natural Rights Theories*, 19; see also S. Thomas de Aquino, *Summa theologiae* Ia–IIae, q. 66, a. 2.

30. See Tuck, *Natural Rights Theories*, 21–22.

31. Duns Scotus, *Quaestiones in librum Sententiarum*, d. 15, q. 2, nr. 3, in *Joannis Duns Scoti Opera Omnia*, vols. V–X (Lyon, 1639; reprint Hildesheim: Olms, 1968), 256–57: "Lege naturae vel divina, non sunt rerum distincta dominia pro statu innocentiae, immo tunc omnia sunt communia. . . . Ratio ad hoc duplex est: Prima, quia usus rerum secundum rectam rationem ita debet competere hominibus, sicut congruit ad congruam et pacificam conversationem, et necessariam sustentationem; in statu autem innocentiae communis usus sine distinctione dominorum ad utrumque istorum plus valuit, quam distinctio dominiorum, quia nullus tunc occupasset quot fuisset alii necessarium, nec oportuisset illud ab ipso per violentiam extorqueri, sed quilibet hoc quod primo occurrisset necessarium, occupasset ad necessarium usum." See Tuck, *Natural Rights Theories*, 21.

32. Tuck, *Natural Rights Theories*, 22: "The Franciscan theory had a normative point: if it was possible for some men to live in an innocent way, then it should be possible for all men to do so. The papacy under John XXII retreated from this radicalism; but in the process it evolved what was to be in the long run the equally radical doctrine of full natural rights. The early fourteenth century saw in this respect a curious anticipation of what was to happen three hundred years later, when natural rights theories were

developed by conservative thinkers as a defence of property, competition and other related values."

33. Ibid., 22–23.

34. Ibid., 25–26.

35. Ibid., 26–27: "It was the first time that an account of a *ius* as a *facultas* had been given. The idea of a *facultas*, an *ability*, had belonged hitherto mainly to non-moral discourse. . . . He [Gerson] was able to make a further move of great importance. I have already stressed that for neither the Romans nor the early medieval lawyers could liberty be a *ius*, a *right*. The Romans had in fact contrasted *libertas* with ius, and emphasised its natural, non-moral character. . . . But by claiming that *ius* was a *facultas*, Gerson was able to assimilate *ius* and *libertas*. As he said in another work, his *Definitiones Terminorum Theologiae Moralis* (written between 1400 and 1415), '*Ius* is a *facultas* or power appropriate to someone and in accordance with the dictates of right reason. *Libertas* is a *facultas* of the reason and will towards whatever possibility is selected. . . . *Lex* is a practical and right reason according to which the movements and workings of things are directed towards their ordained ends.' He was thus even able to make that distinction between *ius* and *lex* which seventeenth-century natural rights theorists thought they had invented." Jean Gerson's texts on which Tuck bases his judgment are Iohannes Gerson, *De Vita Spirituali Animae*, lectio 3, in Iohannes Gerson, *Oeuvres Complètes*, III, edited by Palémon Glorieux (Paris: Desclée, 1962), 141–42: "Jus est facultas seu potestas propinqua conveniens alicui secundum dictamen rectae rationis. . . . Ponitur 'facultas seu potestas,' quoniam multa conveniunt secundum dictamen rectae rationis aliquibus quae non dicuntur jura eorum, ut poena damnatorum, et punitiones viatorum; non enim dicimus aliquem jus habere ad ejus nocumentum. Tamen non est penitus alienum a Scriptura Sacra quod ea dicantur jura quae divina providentia sapientior ordinat, sicut I Reg. dicitur quod hoc erit jus regis, etc. Et daemones dicimus habere jus ad punitionem damnatorum. Ponitur 'propinqua' quoniam multa possunt alicui competere secundum dictamen rectae rationis . . . ut existens actualiter in peccato mortali habet potestatem seu facultatem merendi vitam aeternam, non tamen propinquam vel, ut dici solet, non secundum praesentem justiciam. . . . Dicamus ergo quod omne ens positivum quantum habet de entitate et ex consequenti de bonitate, tantumdem habet de jure sic generaliter definito. In hunc modum coelum jus habet ad influendum, sol ad illuminandum, ignis ad calefaciendum, hirundo ad nidificandum,

immo et quaelibet creatura in omni eo quod bene agere naturali potest facultate. Cujus ratio perspicua est: quoniam omnia talia conveniunt eis secundum dictamen rectae rationis divinae, alioquin nunquam persisterent. Sic homo etiam peccato jus habet ad multa sicut et aliae creaturae naturis suis derelictae. . . . Contractior tamen est ejus acceptio apud polizantes, ut jus dicatur solum de illis quae competunt creturis rationalibus ut utuntur ratione"; and Iohannis Gerson, *Definitiones Terminorum Theologiae Moralis*, in Gerson, *Oeuvres Complètes*, IX, edited by Palémon Glorieux (Paris: Desclée, 1973), 134: "Jus est facultas seu potestas competens alicui secundum dictamen rectae rationis. Libertas est facultas rationis, et voluntatis ad utrumlibet oppositorum. . . . Lex est recta ratio practica secundum quam motus et operationes rerum in suos fines ordinatae regulantur."

36. See Tuck, *Natural Rights Theories*, 27–29.

37. John Finnis, *Natural Law and Natural Rights* (Oxford: Oxford University Press, [1980] 2011).

38. See Brian Tierney, "Natural Law and Natural Rights: Old Problems and Recent Approaches," *Review of Politics* 64 (2002): 389–406; John Finnis, "Aquinas on *ius* and Hart on Rights: A Response to Tierney," *Review of Politics* 64 (2002): 407–10.

39. See Tierney, "Natural Law and Natural Rights," 391–95. Tierney's opinions about Aquinas are assumed and developed in Kenneth Pennington, "*Lex naturalis* and *Ius naturale*," *Jurist* 68 (2008): 569–91, revised and reprinted in *Crossing Boundaries at Medieval Universities*, edited by Spencer E. Young (Leiden: Brill, 2011), 227–53.

40. See Finnis, "Aquinas on *ius* and Hart on Rights," 408–10.

41. See Finnis, *Natural Law and Natural Rights*, 24–25. Finnis considers crucial for contemporary discourse on natural law and natural rights the medieval theories of natural law and mainly of Aquinas's doctrine. This is clearly evident in his entry "Natural Law Theories," in *Stanford Encyclopedia of Philosophy* (Stanford, CA: Center for the Study of Language and Information, 2011), on-line at http://plato.stanfors.edu/archives/fall2011/entries/natural-law-theories/. For a presentation of Finnis's philosophical account on natural law in the history of this concept, see Pauline C. Westerman, *The Disintegration of Natural Law: Aquinas to Finnis* (Leiden: Brill, 1998), 231–85.

42. See Germain G. Grisez, "The First Principle of Practical Reason: A Commentary on the *Summa Theologiae*, 1–2, Question 94, Article 2," *Natural Law Forum* 10 (1965): 168–201. Grisez opens his essay: "My main

purpose is not to contribute to the history of natural law, but to clarify Aquinas's idea of it for current thinking. Instead of undertaking a general review of Aquinas's entire natural law theory, I shall focus on the first principle of practical reason, which also is the first precept of natural law. This principle, as Aquinas states it, is: *Good is to be done and pursued, and evil is to be avoided*. Although verbally this formula is only slightly different from that of the command, *Do good and avoid evil*, I shall try to show that the two formulae differ considerably in meaning and that they belong in different theoretical contexts" (168). Finnis, *Natural Law and Natural Rights*, 24–25, follows Grisez and approaches the subject of natural law from a strictly philosophical point of view: "Since I have yet to show that there are indeed any principles of natural law, let me put the point conditionally. Principles of this sort would hold good, as principles, however extensively they were overlooked, misapplied, or defied in practical thinking, and however little they were recognized by those who reflectively theorize about human thinking. That is to say, they would 'hold good' just as the mathematical principles of accounting 'hold good' even when, as in the medieval banking community, they are unknown or misunderstood. So there could be a history of the varying extent to which they have been used by people, explicitly or implicitly, to regulate their personal activities. There could also be a history of the varying extent to which reflective theorists have acknowledged the sets of principles as valid or 'holding good'. And there could be a history of the popularity of the various theories offered to explain the place of those principles in the whole scheme of things. But of natural law itself there could, strictly speaking, be no history. Natural law could not rise, decline, be revived, or stage 'eternal returns'. It could not have historical achievements to its credit. It could not be held responsible for disasters of the human spirit or atrocities of human practice. But there is a history of the opinions or set of opinions, theories, and doctrines which assert that there are principles of natural law, a history of origins, rises, declines and falls, revivals and achievements, and of historical responsibilities. . . . This book is about natural law. It expounds or sets out a theory of natural law, but is not *about* that theory. Nor is it about other theories. It refers to other theories only to illuminate the theory expounded here, or to explain why some truths about natural law have at various times and in various ways been overlooked or obscured." On Grisez's studies on natural law, see the series of essays collected in *The Revival of Natural Law: Philosophical, Theological and Ethical Responses to the Finnis-Grisez School*, edited by Nigel Biggar and Rufus Black (Aldershot: Ashgate, 2000); see in particular Rufus Black, "Introduction: The New Natural Law Theory," 1–25; Timothy Chappell, "Natural Law Revived: Natural Law Theory and Contemporary Moral Philosophy," 29–52; Ralph McInerny, "Grisez and Thomism," 53–72; Rufus Black, "Is the New Natural Law Theory Christian?," 148–62; Michael Northcott, "The Moral Standing of Nature and the New Natural Law," 262–81.

43. See Finnis, *Natural Law and Natural Rights*, 42–43.

44. S. Thomae de Aquino, *Summa theologiae* IIa–IIae, q. 57, art. 1c, ad 1, ad 2. And see Finnis, *Natural Law and Natural Rights*, 206.

45. Finnis, *Natural Law and Natural Rights*, 206–8.

46. Ibid., 27–49.

47. John Finnis, *Aquinas: Moral, Political, and Legal Theory* (Oxford: Oxford University Press, 1998).

48. Ibid., 133: "The word *ius* (which can be spelled *jus* and is the root of 'just', 'justice', 'juridical', 'inquiry', etc.) has a variety of quite distinct though related meanings. When Aquinas says that *ius* is the object of justice, he means: what justice is about, and what doing justice secures, is the *right* of some other person or persons—what is due to them, what they are entitled to, what is rightfully theirs." In the following lines Finnis develops his analysis showing the connection of this meaning with the contents of the Roman legal tradition.

49. Ibid., 134: "Indeed, the major complication in the semantic of *ius* is that it has also the distinct meaning: law (and thus laws {iura}). Aquinas often uses it with that meaning."

50. Ibid., 134–35: "These two meanings of *ius*—right(s) and law(s)—are rationally connected. To say that someone has a right is to make a claim about what practical reasonableness requires of somebody (or everybody) else. But one's practical reasonableness is guided and shaped by principles and norms, in the first instance by the principles of natural reason, i.e., of natural law—*lex naturalis* or, synonymously, *ius naturale*—and then by any relevant and authoritative rules which have given to natural law some specific *determinatio* for a given community: positive law, i.e., *lex positiva* or, synonymously, *ius positivum*, usually *ius civile*. So, if I have a natural—as we would now say, human—right I have it by virtue of natural law {ius naturale}; if I have a legal right I have it by virtue of positive law {ius positivum}, usually the law specifically of my own state {ius civile}. Thus law, natural or positive, is the basis for one's right(s) {ratio iuris}, precisely because the proposition '*X* has such-and-such a right' cannot

rationally be other than a conclusion form, or a *determinatio* of, practical reason's principles."

51. Ibid., vii.

## *Chapter 3*
## The Long Road to a Common Lexicon

1. In recent years Tierney has made several contributions to the study of John Locke's doctrine of natural rights and its position in the history of natural rights. See in particular Brian Tierney, "Historical Roots of Modern Rights: Before Locke and After," *Ave Maria Law Review* 3 (2005): 23–43; "Dominion of Self and Natural Rights before Locke and After," in *Transformations in Medieval and Early-Modern Rights Discourse*, edited by Virpi Mäkinen and Petter Korkman (Dordrecht: Springer, 2006), 173–203; "Corporatism, Individualism, and Consent: Locke and Premodern Thought," in *Law as Profession and Practice in Medieval Europe: Essays in Honor of James A. Brundage*, edited by Kenneth Pennington and Melodie H. Eichbauer (Farnham: Ashgate, 2011), 49–71. Tierney summarized his position in his reply to Adam Seagrave's critics; see Brian Tierney, "Response to S. Adam Seagrave's 'How Old Are Modern Rights? On the Lockean Roots of Contemporary Human Rights Discourse,'" *Journal of the History of Ideas* 72 (2011): 461–68.

2. Tierney, "Corporatism, Individualism, and Consent," 71. See also Tierney, "Historical Roots," 40.

3. Tierney, "Corporatism, Individualism, and Consent," 71 n. 88. See also Tierney, "Historical Roots," 40–41; Tierney, "Dominion of Self and Natural Rights before Locke and After," 199.

4. One significant example is that of the notion of "permissive natural law." Locke explains that natural law can be seen as the grant for human freedom. John Locke, *Two Treatises of Government*, a critical edition by Peter Laslett (Cambridge: Cambridge University Press, 1960), 287: "To understand Political Power right, and derive it from its Original, we must consider what State all Men are naturally in, and that is, a *State of perfect Freedom* to order their Actions, and dispose of their Possessions, and Persons as they think fit, within the bounds of the Law of Nature, without asking leave, or depending upon the Will of any other Man" (original emphasis). See also Locke, *Two Treatises of Government*, 370. Tierney, "Modern Rights," 37–38, annotates this passage: "In writing like this,

Locke was again adhering to an old tradition of thought, one in which natural law was not seen as opposed to human freedom but as defining it. The ideas of natural law and natural rights had coexisted harmoniously enough for centuries before Locke. From the twelfth century onward, it was commonly held that natural law did not only command and forbid, but also left to humans a wide range of discretionary behavior where they were free to choose their own courses of action and had a right to act as they chose. . . . The idea of a permissive natural law first emerged in the writings of twelfth-century canonists who commented on Gratian's *Decretum* when they considered the origin of individual property." The reference is to a series of decretists who speak of *ius naturale* as absence of prohibition, i.e., as "permissive natural law." For instance, a passage of the *Summa, In nomine* explains this idea; Stephan Kuttner, *Repertorium der Kanonistik (1140–1234): Prodromus Corporis glossarum* (Vatican City: Biblioteca Apostolica Vaticana, 1937; reprinted 1981), 202: "Secundo modo dicitur ius naturale licitum et approbatum quod nec a Domino nec constitutione aliqua precepitur prohibiturve, quod et fas appellatur, ut repetere suum vel non repetere, comedere vel non comedere, dimittere uxorem infidelem cohabitare volentem vel non dimittere. . . . Unde (supra) illud Apostoli 'omnia mihi licent' Ambrosius: lege nature." The author of the *Distinctiones Bambergensis* shares the same doctrine and lists a specific meaning of *ius naturale* among the series of meanings of this lemma. See Rudolf Weigand, *Die Naturrechtslehre der Legisten und Dekretisten von Irnerius bis Accursius und von Gratian bis Johannes Teutonicus* (Munich: M. Hueber, 1967), 205: "Ius naturale . . . quarto modo licitum est et approbatum, quamuis nulla constitutione sit preceptum nec prohibitum ueluti . . . comedere, non comedere, de quo apostolus Paulus cum de usu ciborum loqueretur ut de idolatrio dixit: 'Omnia michi licent', omnia dixit que ad cibum pertinent licent potestate liberi arbitrii et lege naturali, non doctrina legali, quia in lege prohibitum erat ne quis ydolatriis uersceretur." See on this, Tierney, *The Idea of Natural Rights*, 67, 142–43.

5. See Tierney, *The Idea of Natural Rights*, 7.

6. Particularly significant for the study of the history of the idea of natural rights is Brian Tierney, "Origins of Natural Rights Language: Texts and Contexts, 1150–1250," *History of Political Thought* 10 (1989): 615–46, reprinted in Brian Tierney, *Rights, Laws and Infallibility in Medieval Thought* (Aldershot: Variorum, 1997), II.

7. See Brian Tierney, "Tuck on Rights: Some Medieval Problems," *History of Political Thought* 4 (1983): 429–41; Brian Tierney, "Villey,

Ockham, and the Origin of Individual Rights," in *The Weightier Matters of the Law: A Tribute to Harold J. Berman*, edited by John Witte, Frank S. Alexander, and Harold J. Berman (Atlanta: Scholars Press, 1988), 1–31. "Villey, Ockham, and the Origin of Individual Rights" is reprinted in Tierney, *The Idea of Natural Rights*, 13–42.

8. See Tierney, "Origins of Natural Rights Language," 623–24; Tierney, *The Idea of Natural Rights*, 30–34.

9. See Tierney, "Origins of Natural Rights Language," 624–25.

10. In a sort of conclusion to his analysis of Ockham's doctrine about natural law and natural rights, Tierney clearly presents the canonistic doctrine as Ockham's main source. Tierney, *The Idea of Natural Rights*, 202: "The core ideas around which Ockham built his doctrine of natural rights and natural law are genuine canonistic ones, not Ockhamist innovations or distortions. His basic understanding of a right as something that a person could not be deprived of 'without fault or cause' was taken directly from the ordinary glosses to the *Decretum* and the *Decretals*. His three modes of natural law were all anchored in the texts of the *Decretum*. Ockham's teaching on the natural right to use another's property in case of necessity was a standard canonistic doctrine. His insistence that humans were by nature free and not slaves reflected an ancient Stoic teaching, but Ockham again found his authority for it in a text of the *Decretum* and its gloss."

11. See Tierney, "Origins of Natural Rights Language," 628.

12. Ibid., 629.

13. Ibid. The reference is here to the opening lines of Gratian's *Decretum*, where he explains that natural law (*ius naturale*) is contained in the scriptures. See Gratian, *Decretum*, dist. 1, *dictum ante* c. 1, in *Corpus Iuris Canonici*, edited by Emil Friedberg, 2 vols. (Leipzig: B. Tauchnitz, 1879), 1:2.

14. Tierney, "Origins of Natural Rights Language," 629–34; Tierney, *The Idea of Natural Rights*, 58–69.

15. See Tierney, *The Idea of Natural Rights*, 63–64.

16. Ibid., 72–73.

17. Ibid., 77: "The medieval concern for subjective rights in practical everyday life reshaped the language in which discourse about natural right was conducted. By around 1200 many canonists were coming to realize that the old language of *ius naturale* could be used to define both a faculty or force of the human person and a "neutral sphere of personal choice," "a zone of human autonomy." But they did not, like some modern critics of rights theories, expect such language to justify a moral universe in

which each individual would ruthlessly pursue his own advantage. Like most of the theorists down to Locke and Wolff they envisaged a sphere of natural rights bounded by a natural moral law. The first natural rights theories were not based on an apotheosis of simple greed or self-serving egotism; rather they derived from a view of individual human persons as free, endowed with reason, capable of moral discernment, and form a consideration of the ties of justice and charity that bound individuals to one another." The American scholar gave the same conclusion in his "Origins of Natural Rights Language," 644.

18. Brian Tierney, "Natural Rights in the Thirteenth Century: A *Quaestio* of Henry of Ghent," *Speculum* 67 (1992): 58–68, reprinted in Tierney, *The Idea of Natural Rights*, 78–89.

19. See Tierney, *The Idea of Natural Rights*, 88–89.

20. See Tierney, "Dominion of Self and Natural Rights before Locke and After," 199; Tierney, "Corporatism, Individualism, and Consent," 71.

21. Tierney, *The Idea of Natural Rights*, 196–99.

22. Ibid., 169.

23. Ibid., 118–30; Brian Tierney, "The Idea of Natural Rights Origins and Persistence," *Northwestern Journal of International Human Rights* 2 (2004): 1–13, 9.

24. Tierney, *The Idea of Natural Rights*, 197.

25. See Brian Tierney, "Conciliarism, Corporatism, and Individualism: The Doctrine of Subjective Rights in Gerson," *Cristianesimo nella storia* 9 (1988): 81–110, reprinted in Tierney, *The Idea of Natural Rights*, 207–35.

26. About Gerson's influence on the successive fifteenth- and sixteenth-century theorists of natural rights, see Tierney, *The Idea of Natural Rights*, ch. 10 (236–54), devoted to the figures Almain, Mair, and Summenhart; and chs. 11 (255–87) and 12 (288–315), which concern Vitoria, Suárez, and Las Casas. An account of the long chain of which Gerson is a crucial link is offered in Tierney, "Dominion of Self and Natural Rights before Locke and After," 179–98.

27. Tierney, *The Idea of Natural Rights*, 233: "Gerson's achievement should not be underestimated. In pursuing the aims of a whole generation of church reformers, he formulated a theory of individual subjective rights that included a natural right of each person to fulfil God's law, a natural right to liberty, a natural right to self-defense, a natural right to the necessities of life. Moreover these doctrines were not forgotten. Transmitted

by writers like Almain and Soto and Vitoria and Suárez they entered the mainstream of early modern thought on natural rights and so influenced the whole subsequent development of Western political theory."

28. Ibid., 235.

29. On Grotius's importance in the development of natural rights language, see Tierney, *The Idea of Natural Rights*, ch. 13 (316–42). Here Tierney notes, "Like Gerson, Grotius was deploying old arguments, not only in a new idiom, but also in a changed context where they took on new meanings and found a new significance. Grotius was in fact using the medieval tradition of thought about natural law and natural rights to sustain a new vision of the world and the church" (339).

*Chapter 4*
BREAKS, CONTINUITIES, AND SHIFTS

1. Cary J. Nederman, "Review of Brian Tierney, *The Idea of Natural Rights: Studies on Natural Rights, Natural Law and Church Law, 1150–1625*, and *Rights, Law and Infallibility in Medieval Thought*," *American Journal of Legal History* 42 (1998): 217–19; Charles J. Reid, "The Medieval Origins of the Western Natural Rights Tradition: The Achievement of Brian Tierney," *Cornell Law Review* 83 (1998): 437–63.

2. Nederman explains his position mainly in two essays: Cary J. Nederman, "Conciliarism and Contitutionalism: Jean Gerson and Medieval Political Thought," *History of European Ideas* 12 (1990): 189–209; and "Constitutionalism—Medieval and Modern: Against Neo-Figgiste Orthodoxy (Again)," *History of Political Thought* 17 (1996): 179–94.

3. Nederman's criticisms are directed against the idea that late medieval conciliarism could be considered part of the so-called constitutionalism, so that authors such as Pierre d'Ailly and Jean Gerson would be among the founders of modern constitutionalism. Nederman, "Constitutionalism—Medieval and Modern," 182: "My aim is not to diminish the importance of conciliarism as a contribution to Western political thought so much as to place it within its own appropriate context. I do not deny that conciliar theory played an important role in the history of 'constitutionalism', but I insist that conciliarism was a form of constitutional thought and practice deeply rooted in the mental world of the Latin Middle Ages and not directly germane to our own modern political framework and

dilemmas." Nederman, denying the fact that conciliarism is part of constitutionalism, puts in question the basic idea of a cultural continuity in political and legal thought between the Middle Ages and modernity.

4. See Nederman, "Jean Gerson and Medieval Political Thought," 201–2, where he stresses the medieval character of Gerson's political doctrines. According to Nederman, Gerson's writings and ideas belong to the late medieval intellectual framework, whereas "modernity" has completely different features for what concerns ideas such as natural rights. The latter were in fact proper to constitutionalism, which in Nederman's view is an entirely modern political perspective.

5. See Nederman, "Constitutionalism—Medieval and Modern," 183. Here Nederman is quoting from the preface of Quentin Skinner, *The Foundations of Modern Political Thought*, vol. 1 (Cambridge: Cambridge University Press, 1978), x: "The clearest sign that a society has entered into the self-conscious possession of a new concept is, I take it, that a new vocabulary comes to be generated, in terms of which the concept is then articulated and discussed."

6. See Nederman, "Constitutionalism—Medieval and Modern," 194.

7. See Cary Nederman, "Empire and the Historiography of European Political Thought: Marsiglio of Padua, Nicholas of Cusa, and the Medieval-Modern Divide," *Journal of the History of Ideas* 66 (2005): 1–15, 2. Cf. John Pocock, *The Machiavellian Moment: Florentine Political Thought and the Atlantic Republican Tradition* (Princeton, NJ: Princeton University Press, 1975); John Pocock, *Barbarism and Religion*, vol. 3: *The First Decline and Fall* (Cambridge: Cambridge University Press, 2003).

8. S. Adam Seagrave, "How Old Are Modern Rights? On the Lockean Roots of Contemporary Human Rights Discourse," *Journal of the History of Ideas* 72 (2011): 305–27.

9. Ibid., 317: "Two points seem clear: first, medieval rights of the sort Tierney describes are not *rights* in the full or strict sense of individual moral powers with their own justificatory basis; and secondly, modern rights are treated as meaningful in this way precisely because they are viewed apart from a natural law framework or a legislating God" (original emphasis).

10. See Seagrave, "How Old Are Modern Rights?," 318.

11. See Leo Strauss, *Natural Right and History* (Chicago: University of Chicago Press, 1953), 165–66.

12. See S. Adam Seagrave, "Identity and Diversity in the History of Ideas: A Reply to Brian Tierney," *Journal of the History of Ideas* 73 (2012): 163–66.

13. Skinner suggested one further methodological element, together with his attention to the linguistic changes. Considering the evolution of political thought, he stresses the importance of a careful study of the social, cultural, and political context in which specific texts were composed. Thus Skinner remarks on the need to consider together the development of political thought and the changing historical framework. Skinner, *The Foundations of Modern Political Thought*, 1: xi: "I take it that political life itself sets the main problems for the political theorist, causing a certain range of issues to appear problematic, and a corresponding range of questions to become the leading subjects of debate. This is not to say, however, that I treat these ideological superstructures as a straightforward outcome of their social base. I regard it as no less essential to consider the intellectual context in which the major texts were conceived—the context of earlier writings and inherited assumptions about political society, and of more ephemeral contemporary contributions to social and political thought. For it is evident that the nature and limits of the normative vocabulary available at any given time will also help to determine the ways in which particular questions come to be singled out and discussed." Skinner points out that the literary and doctrinal characteristics of a text are deeply connected to the distinctive time and culture in which the author composed it. However, this does not mean that is not possible to take a long perspective, considering the evolution in the history of a concept, a lemma, or an idea. Considering a single author or a single work could cut the cultural links with the previous and following cultural contexts that are crucial to understanding the genesis and the reception of a text and its contents. James H. Burns exemplified this point in his 2008 preface to *The Cambridge History of Medieval Political Thought, c. 350–c. 1450*, edited by James H. Burns (Cambridge: Cambridge University Press, 2008), 4: "Even if the net is cast more widely and the definition of a 'political thinker' made more flexible, so much of the evidence will be lost as to leave the resulting 'history' unacceptably spasmodic and patchy. Whole tracts of time, indeed, would virtually disappear if the record were restricted to the work of individual thinkers. Yet without an understanding of, in particular, the earlier medieval centuries, our perspectives on the later period, with its revival of explicit political discussion and analysis carried out by more readily identifiable 'political thinkers', must be misleadingly foreshortened. To see these later medieval political ideas, in some sense no doubt ideas reflecting a more sophisticated culture, in the context of the earlier sources upon which their exponents continued to draw is, for one thing, to gain a degree

of security against the risk of distortion when what is 'medieval' is viewed and assessed in terms of its supposed anticipation of what is regarded as 'modern.'" The fact that a text and a doctrine could be well understood only with respect to the specific historical features of the time and place and culture to which they belong does not contradict the historical connections between that text and doctrine and the past and future of the history of political thought. In the case of ideas such as natural law and natural right it is particularly clear that their relation to both their sources and their reception is not just complementary to their history, but is an essential part of it.

14. See in particular Tierney, "Response to S. Adam Seagrave's 'How Old Are Modern Rights?'"

15. Francis Oakley, *The Conciliarist Tradition: Constitutionalism in the Catholic Church, 1300–1870* (Oxford: Oxford University Press, 2003).

16. Ibid., 5–6.

17. Francis Oakley, *Natural Law, Law of Nature, Natural Rights: Continuity and Discontinuity in the History of Ideas* (New York: Continuum, 2005).

18. Ibid., 23–26.

19. Oakley remarks on the importance of the changes in the notion of nature for the evolution of the ideas of natural law and natural right. His approach suggests that if "nature" is the basic element of semantic shifts through the centuries, then the understanding of the developments in the history of natural law and natural rights concerns also metaphysics. Oakley, after comparing the changes in the idea of nature to profound geological faults, notes, "The later Middle Ages, I would suggest, can helpfully be understood as a period distinguished, intellectually speaking, by a recrudescence of precisely such seismic activity leading to, among other things, a reconceptualization of the metaphysical grounding of the law of nature in both the moral/juridical order and the order of physical nature." Oakley, *Natural Law, Law of Nature, Natural Rights*, 26–27.

20. Annabel Brett, *Liberty, Right and Nature: Individual Rights in Later Scholastic Thought* (Cambridge: Cambridge University Press, 1997).

21. Annabel Brett, "Scholastic Political Thought and the Modern Concept of the State," in *Rethinking the Foundations of Modern Political Thought*, edited by James Tully and Annabel Brett (Cambridge: Cambridge University Press, 2006), 130–48.

22. Brett, *Liberty, Right and Nature*, 6–7.

23. Ibid., 123–64.

24. See Brett, "Scholastic Political Thought," 131, where she notes the significance of Skinner's remark about the "revival of scholasticism" in sixteenth-century political thought. See Skinner, *The Foundations of Modern Political Thought*, 1:135–73. Skinner's focus on scholasticism as one of the sources of modern political thought rests on the idea that the birth of "modernity" is not reducible to the dichotomy between (medieval) scholasticism and (modern) humanism. Brett, "Scholastic Political Thought," 131: "Instead of a simple dichotomy between humanism and scholasticism, Skinner consistently insisted on a triad of scholasticism, humanism and the heritage of Roman law in the developments he was interested in. Again, he did not associate Renaissance political thought exclusively with humanist political thought, and he stretched both back to the thirteenth century, well beyond previously defined and celebrated contours. The Reformation remained the Reformation, but has its roots in fourteenth- and fifteenth-century critiques of the papacy. In the case of constitutionalism, Skinner relocates the origin of the most popular forms of constitutionalism in Catholic rather than Calvinist circles."

25. Brett explains her perspective on the issues of natural law and natural rights in the introduction to her 1997 volume. Brett, *Liberty, Right and Nature*, 7: "This book, therefore, is not an attempt to find the origin for the, or any, modern concept of subjective right. What I try to do instead is to recover the variety of the senses of the term *ius* as employed to signify a quality or property of the individual subject in late mediaeval and renaissance scholastic discourse. The reassessment of *ius* in a subjective sense entails that its relation with the notion of objective right be reconsidered: I therefore attempt to assess the precise understanding of objective right held by authors of this period. To escape the grip of the philosophical history of subjective right sketched earlier, I try to get behind the categories of voluntarist, nominalist, realist and the like, which have too often shaded over into explanatory factors, and concentrate instead on the nature of the literature in which *ius* is used in a subjective sense, taking into account the constraints of genre within scholastic literary production."

26. See in particular Tierney, *The Idea of Natural Rights*, 99–100, where he notes that Ockham focused not only on the concept of divine omnipotence and free will. The Franciscan master had stressed the importance of "right reason" in moral agency. "Right reason" is the basic element of the foundation of his doctrine of natural law and natural rights, since the *ius naturale* is presented precisely as "force of reason." According to Ockham, it is self-evident that will ought to act in conformity with right

reason. Guillelmus de Ockham, *Quodlibet II*, q. 14, art. 3, in *Guillelmi de Ockham Opera Philosophica et Theologica, IX*, cura Instituti Franciscani Universittatis S. Bonaventurae (New York: St. Bonaventure University, 1980), 177: "multa sunt principia per se nota in morali philosophia; puta quod voluntas debet se conformare rectae rationi, omne malum vituperabile est fugiendum et huiusmodi."

27. Sten Gagnér, "Vorbemerkung zum Thema 'Dominium' bei Ockham," *Miscellanea mediaevalia* 9 (1974): 293–327. Cf. Tierney, *The Idea of Natural Rights*, 100–101.

28. See Tierney, *The Idea of Natural Rights*, 102–3. Tierney notes that even if Ockham remains a theologian, he acquired a consistent legal culture through his dispute with John XXII. Furthermore, the dispute with the pope concerned the legal understanding of the notions of property and rights, so that this, Tierney suggests, could explain why Ockham focused on a legal and political perspective rather than on a philosophical and theological one. The great "classics" of the canonistic tradition, namely, the *Decretum* with its ordinary glosses and the *Decretals*, would have provided him with the essential doctrinal and cultural sources. So, Tierney notes, "Ockham was not striving to construct a political theory or a system of ecclesiology in a vacuum. He was engaged in a furious dispute with the pope. His own positions were shaped in response to the arguments, often juridical arguments, of the enemies he sought to vanquish" (103).

29. Tierney, *The Idea of Natural Rights*, 130.

30. Brett, *Liberty, Right and Nature*, 51: "I shall argue that Ockham's understanding of *ius* as a *potestas* is not the same as that of the earlier Franciscan literature. *Ius* in Ockham is integrated into a quite different philosophy of agency, one which does not use the dichotomy between nature and spirit and one which therefore need not assimilate *ius* to liberty or to *dominium* in the strong sense."

31. Ibid., 64–65.

32. Michel Bastit, *Naissance de la loi moderne* (Paris: Presses Universitaires de France, 1990).

33. Ibid., 50: "Saint Thomas entreprend d'abord de dégager une notion de loi réalisée à travers diverses expériences juridiques, religieuses, morales, que l'homme peut faire de cette réalité. Il ne s'agit aucunement de rechercher une idée de loi existant en dehors de lois particulières et des réalités diverses qui sont actuellement régis par des lois, mais de recherche ce qui est l'essence de cette diversité, quoique n'existant pas en dehors des loi particulières où cette notion est réalisée. On ne retournera pas vers les

lois particulières par un processus de divions de plus en plus restreinte de cette notion commune, on constatera au contraire très rapidement la diversité de cette réalisation."

34. Ibid., 220–26.

35. Bastit's summary of the development of the history of the notion of natural law is clearly inspired by Villey. See Bastit, *Naissance de la loi moderne*, 361–76. He points out the importance of the break caused by Duns Scotus and Ockham, with their nominalism, in the development of an idea of "natural law" grounded in reality and in the metaphysical order of the world: "Au cours de l'histoire de cette très profonde transformation en laquelle consiste la naissance de la loi moderne, le rôle décisif est tenu par les philosophies à la fois si contraires et si complémentaires de Jean Duns Scot et de Guillaume d'Occam. Ce sont elles qui rompent brutalement et définitivement avec la conception analogique de la loi pour la remplacer par une notion de la loi univoque, qui doit, jusqu'au plus bas échelon, s'applique uniformément. Par là se manifeste le très profond volontarisme de ces pensées. Duns Scot privilégie l'abstraction formelle au point de substituer ses produits à la réalité, il laisse cependant échapper à son système de formes la matière, et dans une certaine mesure l'individu, qui fournissent à leur tour le fondement sur lequel Occam base une théologie de la toute-puissance qui lui permet de réduire la réalité à un chaos de faits bruts. Pour donner son complet essor à la loi moderne, Suarez n'aura plus qu'à développer une dialectique des formes et de la matière, déjà présente à l'état germinatif chez Scot. Il lui suffira de montrer que le singulier est un simple mode de l'universel, qui peut donc prétendre légitimement à enserrer toute la réalité, sauf à ce que l'on puisse aussi dans la ligne d'Occam réduire inversement l'universel au singulier. . . . L'observation du processus historique de constitution de cette conception moderne de la loi met alors en pleine lumière les contradictions qui la soustendent" (362–63).

36. Arthur Stephen McGrade, "Natural Law and Moral Omnipotence," in *The Cambridge Companion to Ockham*, edited by Paul Vincent Spade (Cambridge: Cambridge University Press, 1999), 273–301.

37. Oakley, *Natural Law, Laws of Nature, Natural Rights*, 24.

38. Ibid., 35–62.

39. Brian Tierney, "*Natura id est Deus*: A Case of Juristic Pantheism?," *Journal of the History of Ideas* 24 (1963): 307–22, reprinted in Brian Tierney, *Church Law and Constitutional Thought in the Middle Ages* (London: Variorum, 1979), no. VII.

40. Kenneth Pennington, *The Prince and the Law, 1200–1600: Sovereignty and Rights in the Western Legal Tradition* (Berkeley: University of California Press, 1993), esp. ch. 4, "Natural Law and Positive Law: Due Process and the Prince," 119–64. Pennington also offers a detailed analysis of the influence of Roman law in twelfth-century culture in his "The *Big Bang:* Roman Law in the Early Twelfth-Century," *Rivista internazionale di diritto comune* 18 (2007): 43–70.

41. Ennio Cortese, *La norma giuridica: Spunti teorici nel diritto comune classico*, 2 vols. (Milan: Giuffrè Editore, 1962–64).

42. Rudolf Weigand, *Die Naturrechtslehre der Legisten und Dekretisten von Irnerius bis Accursius und von Gratian bis Johannes Teutonicus* (Munich: M. Hueber, 1967), 443–46.

43. For the contribution of Calasso, see Francesco Calasso, *Medio evo del diritto, I: Le fonti* (Milan: Giuffrè Editore, 1954); and *I glossatori e la teoria della sovranità: Studio di diritto comune pubblico* (Milan: Giuffrè Editore, 1951). For a discussion of the importance of Calasso's studies and of the relations between the Italian scientific milieu and the international debate, see Emanuele Conte, "Droit médiéval: Un débat historiographique italien," *Annales. Histoire. Sciences Sociales* 57 (2002): 1593–1613; Emanuele Conte, "Storia interna e storia esterna: Il diritto medievale da Francesco Calasso alla fine del XX secolo," *Rivista internazionale di diritto comune* 17 (2006): 299–322.

44. Paolo Grossi, *L'ordine giuridico medievale*, new ed. (Rome, 2011).

45. Ibid., 80–85.

46. See Guarnerius Iurisperitissimus, *Liber divinarum sententiarum*, edited by Giuseppe Mazzanti (Spoleto: Centro Italiano di studi sull'alto Medioevo, 1999).

47. Andrea Padovani, *Perché chiedi il mio nome? Dio natura e diritto nel secolo XII* (Turin: Giappichelli, 1997), 20–25, 254–71.

48. Ibid., 272–76.

49. Ibid., 67–86.

Chapter 5
HIGHLIGHTS AND SHADOWS OF A PORTRAIT

1. Merio Scattola has offered a useful synthesis of the main features of the medieval approach to natural law and natural rights. He identified six characteristics of the medieval idea of natural law: (1) it is a set of innate

rules; (2) it corresponds to the Ten Commandments; (3) it includes a plurality of independent principles and rules; (4) it is part of the universal order of justice that governs the whole of creation (the superior, universal order in which all of the existing rules play a role can be rationally reconstructed by that human mind and it is an objective order with respect to which it is possible to evaluate good and evil in an objective sense; and the superior order is not immediately visible and pertains to the eternal law that is superior to all human laws and knowledge); (5) it contains rules that are immediately in force in civil society; (6) it and the law of nations are two different kinds of law that are not organized hierarchically (the former is the rational behavior of human beings; the latter is a set of rights and duties organized by human reason through discourse). See Merio Scattola, "Models in History of Natural Law," *Ius commune: Zeitschrift für Europäische Rechtsgeschichte* 28 (2001): 91–159.

2. *Dig.* I.1.3: "Ius naturale est quod natura omnia animalia docuit. Nam ius istud non humani generis proprium, sed omnium animalium quae in terra, quae in mari nascuntur, avium quoque commune est. Hinc descendit maris atque foeminae coniunctio, quam nos matrimonium appellamus: hinc liberorum procreatio, hinc educatio. Videmus etenim caetera quoque animalia, feras etiam istius iuris peritia censeri." The English translation is quoted from *The Digest of Justinian*, edited by Charles Henry Monro and William Warwick Buckland (Cambridge: Cambridge University Press, 1904), 3.

3. As Irnerius himself writes in a short note, "natura enim nichil priuatum." See Enrico Besta, *L'opera d'Irnerio (Contributo alla storia del diritto italiano)* (Turin: Arnaldo Forni Editore, 1896), 3.

4. Irnerius, *Glossa* to *Dig.* 1.1.1.3: "A natura enim permittitur ut iungantur et socientur." Rudolf Wiegand, *Die Naturrechtslehre der Legisten und Dekretisten von Irnerius bis Accursius und von Gratian bis Johannes Teutonicus* (Munich: M. Hueber, 1967), 18.

5. Irnerius explains this "teaching" role of "nature" in several glosses. *Dig.* 1, 1, 1, 3: "Diuini prodita generaliter et singulatim"; *Inst.* 1, 2, pr.: "Diuina prodita iudicio generaliter, singulariter indidit nature ciuium"; and most extensively *Inst.* 1, 2, pr.: "Est enim in omnibus natura prodita diuino iudicio qua docemur cuncta hec agere sine doctrina; quod ergo illa natura docet, ius dicitur naturale a natura docente illud." All passages are quoted from Weigand, *Naturrechtslehre*, 18–19.

6. *Summa institutionum Vindobonensis*, III, 1: "Ius naturale est conditio rebus creatis ab ipsa divina dispositione imposita, seu instinctu

nature, non aliqua constitutione. Non enim ex hominum industria, sed ex ipsa divina dispositione est inductum. Est enim ius quod natura omnia docuit animalia, cuius iuris peritia omnia censentur animalia. Hinc descendit maris et femine coniugatio, quam, secuta quadam sollemnitate, inter nos matrimonium appellamus. Hinc liberorum procreatio et educatio. Que quidem non iura, sed iuris effectus dicuntur." In Weigand, *Naturrechtslehre*, 27.

7. *Inst.* 1, 2: "Ius naturale aliud generale quod pertinet omnibus animalibus, aliud speciale quod pertinet hominibus tantum quod etiam uocatur ius gentium." In Weigand, *Naturrechtslehre*, 34.

8. Martinus, *Inst.* 1,1: "Ius autem sic diffinitur 'ars boni et equi'. Hec diffinitio et iuri naturli, gentium et ciuili competit. Ius enim naturale cum sit constitutio diuine uoluntatis, potest dici ars boni et equi. A tali constitutione procedit coniugatio maris atque femine et multa alia que iura non dicuntur set effectus iuris. Item ius gentium cum sit constitutio rationis a natura in anima insite ars dicitur boni et equi, set cum quadam distinctione. Hec enim constitutio, scilicet quod quisque ob tutelam sui corporis fecerit, iure fecisse dicitur, quippe huius orationis significatum naturalis ratio constituit, constituta est de bono, ita quod de equo." In Weigand, *Naturrechtslehre*, 32. The legist repeats his opinion glossing *Inst.* 1, 2, 11: "Appellatio naturalis iuris alia significat secundum naturam animalem, alias secundum naturalem rationem; hic autem significat secundum specialem naturam rationis. Ius gentium ideo uocat naturale, quia naturali equitate et ratione processit." In Weigand, *Naturrechtslehre*, 34.

9. See Ennio Cortese, *La norma giuridica: Spunti teorici nel diritto comune classico*, 2 vols. (Milan: Giuffrè Editore, 1962–64), 1:37–96; Weigand, *Naturrechtslehre*, 17–120; Richard Tuck, *Natural Rights Theories: Their Origin and Development* (Cambridge: Cambridge University Press, 1979); Andrea Padovani, *Perché chiedi il mio nome? Dio natura e diritto nel secolo XII* (Turin: Giappichelli, 1997).

10. See Harold Berman, *Law and Revolution: The Formation of the Western Legal Tradition* (Cambridge, MA: Harvard University Press, 1983); Brian Tierney, *The Idea of Natural Rights: Studies on Natural Rights, Natural Law, and Church Law, 1150–1625* (Atlanta, GA: Scholar Press, 1997); Paolo Prodi, *Una storia della giustizia: Dal pluralismo dei fori al moderno dualismo tra coscienza e diritto* (Bologna: Il Mulino, 2000); Diego Quaglioni, *La giustizia nel Medioevo e nella prima età moderna* (Bologna: Il Mulino, 2004).

11. Gratianus, *Concordantia Discordantium Canonum*, dist. 1, *dictum ante* c.1. in *Corpus Iuris Canonici*, 1:1: "Humanum genus duobus regitur, naturale videlicet iure et moribus. Ius naturale est, quod in lege et Evangelio continetur: quo quisque iubetur alii facere quod sibi vult fieri, et prohibetur alii inferre quod sibi noli fieret." The English translation is quoted from *Gratian: The Treatise on Laws (Decretum DD. 1–20)*, translated by Augustine Thompson, *with the Ordinary Gloss*, translated by James Gordley with an introduction by Katherine Christensen (Washington, DC: Catholic University of America Press, 1993), 3.

12. Gratianus, *Concordantia Discordantium Canonum*, c.7, 2: "Ius naturale est commune omnium nationum eo quod ubique instinctu naturae non constitutione aliqua habetur, ut viri et feminae coniunctio, liberorum successio et educatio, communis omnium possessio, et omnium una libertas, acquisitio eorum quae caelo, terra, marique capiuntur, item depositae rei vel commendatae pecuniae restitutio, violentiae per vim repulsio. Nam hoc, aut si quid huic simile est, numquam iniustum, sed naturale equumque habetur." For the English text, see *Gratian: The Treatise on Laws (Decretum DD. 1–20)*, 6–7.

13. See Padovani, *Perché chiedi il mio nome?*

14. Stephan Kuttner stressed Gratian's knowledge of the philosophical elements of the legal culture of his time. In particular he evidenced how the author of the *Concordantia Discordantium Canonum* was acquainted with Plato's *Timeus* and with Calcidius's commentary. See Stephan Kuttner, "Gratian and Plato," in *Church and Government in the Middle Ages: Essays Presented to C. R. Cheney*, edited by Christopher N. L. Brooke et al. (Cambridge: Cambridge University Press, 1976): 93–118, reprinted in Stephan Kuttner, *History of Ideas and Doctrines of Canon Law in the Middle Ages* (London: Variorum, 1980), no. XI.

15. Rom. 2:13–15.

16. Rom. 13:1–3.

17. See Martin Grabmann, *Die Geschichte der scholastischen Methode*, 2 vols. (Freiburg: Herder, 1909–11); Joseph De Ghellink, *Le mouvement théologique du XIIe siècle: Sa préparation lointaine avant et autour de Pierre Lombard ses rapports avec les initiatives des canonistes. Études, recherches et documents* (Bruges: Ed. Du Temple, 1948); Odon Lottin, *Psychologie et morale aux XIIe et XIIIe siècles*, vol. 5: *Problèmes d'histoire littéraire. L'école d'Anselme de Laon et de Guillaume de Champeaux* (Gembloux: Duculot, 1957); David E. Luscombe, *The School of Peter*

*Abelard: The Influence of Abelard's Thought in the Early Scholastic Period* (Cambridge: Cambridge University Press, 1969); Padovani, *Perché chiedi il mio nome?*; Cédric Giraud, *Per verba magistri: Anselme de Laon et son école au XIIe siècle* (Turnhout: Brepols, 2010).

18. Stephen de Tournai (Stephanus Tornacensis), *Die Summa über das Decretum Gratiani*, edited by Johann F. von Schulte (Giessen: Emil Roth, 1891), 1: "Duos ad convivium vocavi, theologum et legistam, quorum voluntates varia sparguntur in vota, cum iste delectetur acido, ille dulcia concupiscat. Quid demus? Quid non demus? Renuis tu, quod petit alter? Occurrentes in opusculo praesenti leges exponere si proponam, iuris peritus aegere feret, nares contrahet in rugam, caput concutiet, exporriget libellum et, quod sibi notum reputat, aliis non necessarium opinatur. Patrum veteris aut novi testamenti gesta mystica si narrare coepero, sicut inutilia reputabit theologus et opusculum nostrum tum prolixitatis arguet, tum ingratitudinis accusabit." On the definition of a specific epistemological status of the legal discourse, see the studies of Andrea Errera: *Arbor actionum: Genere letterario e forma di classificazione delle azioni nella dottrina dei glossatori* (Bologna: Monduzzi, 1995); and *Lineamenti di epistemologia giuridica medievale. Storia di una rivoluzione scientifica* (Turin: Giappichelli, 2006).

19. See Richard W. Southern, *Scholastic Humanism and the Unification of Europe*, 2 vols. (Oxford: Blackwell, 1995–2001); Marcia Colish, *Medieval Foundations of the Western Intellectual Tradition, 400–1400* (New Haven, CT: Yale University Press, 1998).

20. See Leonard Boyle, "The Inter-Conciliar Period: 1179–1215 and the Beginnings of Pastoral Manuals," in *Miscellanea Rolando Bandinelli Papa Alessandro III*, edited by Filippo Liotta (Siena: Accademia Senese degli Intronati, 1986), 43–56.

21. Colin Morris, *The Discovery of the Individual, 1050–1200* (London: SPCK, 1972). On the importance of the "discovery of the subject" for the preparation of modern culture, see Hans Blumenberg, *Die Legitimität der Neuzeit* (Frankfurt am Main: Suhrkamp Verlag, 1974$^2$).

22. The masters of Laon debated about "natural law" in their biblical glosses, particularly to Rom. 2. See on this Lottin, *Psychologie et morale*, vol. 5, ad indicem.

23. "Ius quippe aliud naturale, aliud positiuum dicitur. Naturale quidem ius est quod opere complendum esse ipsa que omnibus naturaliter inest ratio persuadet, et idcirco apud omnes permanet, ut Deum colere, parentes amare, peruersos punire, et quorumcumque obseruantia ita

omnibus est necessaria ut nulla umquam sine illis merita sufficiant. Positiue autem iustitie illud est quod, ab hominibus institutum ad utilitatem scilicet uel honestatem tutius muniendam uel amplificandam, aut sola consuetudine aut scripti nititur auctoritate." Peter Abelard, *Collationes*, edited by John Marenbon and Giovanni Orlandi (Oxford: Clarendon Press, 2001), 144–46.

24. Abelard suggests the role of natural law as capability to know and love God proper of all human beings, using the example of the Roman centurion Cornelius. The master's words show that even if Cornelius received salvation only by faith in Christ, he knew God before his meeting with St. Peter. Peter Abelard, *Ethica*, in *Petri Abaelardi Opera Theologica, IV: Scito Te Ipsum*, edited by Rainer M. Ilgner (Turnhout: Brepols 2001), $42^{1106}$–$43^{1114}$: "Non credebat Cornelius in Christum, donec Petrus ad eum missus de hoc ipsum instruxit. Qui quamuis antea lege naturali deum recognosceret atque diligeret, ex quo meruit de oracione sua audiri et deo acceptas elemosinas habere, tamen si eum ante fidem Christi de hac luce migrasse contingeret, nequaquam ei uitam promittere auderemus, quantumcunque bona eius opera uiderentur, nec eum fidelibus set magis infidelibus connumeraremus, quantocunque studio inquirende salutis esset occupatus."

25. Accursius, *Glossa ordinaria, Inst.* 1, 2, pr.: "v. natura: et nominatiue et ablatiue, sic supra tit. i. § i. Et nota quod quattuor modis ius naturale ponitur: Quandoque pro iure gentium ut infra de rer. Diui. § Singulorum; quandoque pro iure pactorum ut ff. de pact. l. i.; quandoque pro eius contrario, scilicet pro eo quod rescindit pacta, ut in restitutione minorum, ut ff. de mino. l. i.; quandoque pro instinctu nature ut hic. Secundum canones ius naturale dicitur quod in lege mosaica uel Euangelio continetur, ut in principio decretorum. Et istud, 'quod' hic est nominatiui casus, quando hec dictio 'natura' est ablatiui, et econtra est accusatiui, quando 'natura' est nominatiui, et tunc dic: natura, id est Deus. Acc." In Weigand, *Naturrechtslehre*, 57. Accursius repeats these ideas in the gloss to the *Digest, Dig.* 1.1.1.3: "v. natura: id est Deus et sic nominatiui; uel dic quod sit ablatiui casus. Item nota ius naturale quattuor modis dici. Primo lex Mosaica, ut instit. de obl. ex del. § i. Secundo instictus nature ut hic. Tertio ius gentium ut instit. de rer. diui. § Singulorum. Quarto ius pretorium, ut infra de minor. l. i. et facit, inst, de iure natu. in princ." In Weigand, *Naturrechtslehre*, 57.

26. Accursius, *Glossa ordinaria, Dig.* 2, 14, 1: "v. Huius edicti: . . . et quod dicit 'naturalis', dic id est naturali ingenio uel industria hominum

introducta quod est iurisgentium et sic ponitur ius naturale insti. de rer. Diu. § Singulorum. Proprie autem non significatur nisi ea aequitas, quae communis est omnium animantium ut supra de iusti. et iure l. i. § Ius naturale. Et quia hic naturalis equitas, inducitur naturalis obligatio per pactum." In Wiegand, *Naturrechtslehre*, 61.

27. *Biblia Latina cum glossa ordinaria*, edited by Adophus Rusch, 4 vols. (Strassburg, 1480/81; reprint Turnhout: Brepols, 1992), vol. 4, 278b: "v. Cum enim gentes [2, 14]: Cum enim dixerat gentilem damnari si male operatur, saluari si bene; sed cum legem non habeat, quasi nesciat quid sit bonum quidue malum, uideretur sibi neutrum debere imputari. Contra, Apostolus: etsi non habeat scriptam legem, habet naturalem, quia intelligit et sibi conscius est quid sit bonum et quid sit malum et ideo credendus est bene uel male operari et merito saluari uel damnari. Bene operari dico et saluari quod non est nisi per gratiam et fidem, qua renouat naturalem imaginem Dei in homine ex uicio et uetustate sopita, sine qua renouatione male operatur, et damnatur accusante cum conscientia; uicium quippe contra naturam est quod utique sanat gratia. Non enim usque a Deo in humana anima ymago terrenorum affectuum labe detrita est ut nulla in ea lineamenta remanserint. Non omnino deletum est quod ibi per imaginem Dei cum crearetur impressum est. Proinde uicio sanato per gratiam, naturaliter sunt ea que legis sunt. Non quod per nature nomen negata sit gratia, sed potius per gratiam reparata natura, quam gratia interiori homine renouato lex iusticie rescribitur deleuerat culpa."

28. See Pennington, *"Lex naturalis* and *Ius naturale,"* 228.

29. Ibid., 234–35; Prodi, *Una storia della giustizia*, 54–57; Luscombe, *Peter Abelard's Ethica*, xxvi; John Marenbon, "Abelard's Concept of Natural Law," in *Miscellanea Mediaevalia*, Band 21, 2: *Mensch und Natur im Mittelalter*, edited by Albert Zimmermann (Berlin: Walter de Gruyter, 1992): 609–21.

30. See Peter von Inwagen, "The Nature of Metaphysics," in *Contemporary Readings in the Foundation of Metaphysics*, edited by Stephen Laurence and Cynthia Macdonald (Oxford: Blackwell, 1998), 11–21.

31. See on this the crucial considerations of Marie-Dominique Chenu, *La théologie au XIIe siècle* (Paris: Vrin, 1976): 19–51. See also the essays collected in Tullio Gregory, *Speculum naturale: Percorsi del pensiero medievale* (Rome: Edizioni di Storia e Letteratura, 2007).

32. Particularly influential in the culture of eleventh- and twelfth-century legists and canonists appears to be the series of causes that Eriugena drew in the opening lines of his *Periphyseon*. He wrote: "*Nutritor.* Est igitur

natura generale nomen . . . omnium quae sunt et quae non sunt. . . . Videtur mihi diuisio naturae per quatuor differentias quatuor species recipere, quarum prima est in eam quae creat et non creatur, secunda in eam quae et creatur et creat, tertia in eam quae creatur et non creat, quarta quae nec creat nec creatur. Harum uero quattuor binae sibi inuicem opponuntur. Nam tertia opponitur primae, quarta uero secundae; sed quarta inter impossibilia ponitur, cuius esse est non posse esse. . . . Vides, ni fallor, tertiae speciei primae oppositionem. Prima namque creat et non cretur, cui e contrario opponitur illa quae creatur et non creat; secunda uero quartae, siquidem secunda et creatur et creat, cui uniuersaliter quarta contradicit, quae non creat neque creatur. *Alumnus.* Clare uideo. Sed multum me mouet quarta species quae a te addita est. Nam de aliis tribus nullo modo haesitare ausim, cum prima, ut arbitror, in causa omnium quae sunt, quae deus est, intelligetur; secunda uero in primordialibus causis; tertia in his quae in generatione temporibusque et locis cognoscuntur. Atque ideo de singulis disputari subtilius necessarium est, ut uideo." Iohannes Scotus Eriugena, *Periphyseon*, I, 1, in *Iohannis Scoti seu Eriugenae Periphyseon: Liber Primus*, edited by Édourad Jeauneau (Turnhout: Brepols, 1996), $3^5-4^{39}$. On the influence of Eriugena's metaphysics on the idea of nature of twelfth-century legists and canonists, see Padovani, *Perché chiedi il mio nome?*, 153–76.

33. About the nature and value of *natura id est Deus*, see the synthesis offered in Maria Grazia Fantini, *La cultura del giurista medievale: Natura, causa, ratio* (Rome: Franco Angeli, 1998). Brian Tierney's consideration on the origin and fortune of this formula are still crucial. See Tierney, "*Natura id est Deus*: A Case of Juristic Pantheism?*" Tierney criticizes the analysis of Ugo Gualazzini, "Natura id est Deus," *Studia Gratiana* 3 (1955): 413–24. On the idea of natural law as "equity," see Padovani, *Perché chiedi il mio nome?*, 55–66.

34. The persistence of this "Platonic" idea of nature in thirteenth-century culture is evident in some texts that are used in university courses. The anonymous author of the *Accessus philosophorum*, an introduction to philosophy, notes: "Intentio Platonis in *Thimeo* est ostendere rem publicam esse informandam ad instar naturalis iusticie, quam quidem naturalem iustitiam appellamus dispositionem partium uniuersi. Ordinatio enim partium uniuersi elegantissima est et conuenientissima, sicut patet in moribus corporum superiorum, in compage elementorum et in temporum uarietate, quod, licet diuersi sint motus superiorum corporum, superior tamen non impedit inferiorem, immo regulat et dirigit ipsum et amminiculatur eidem. Similiter elementorum qualitates, quamuis sint repugnantes

et contrarie, tamen conueniunt ad generationem uniuscuiusque rei nec omnino corrumpit unum elementum alterum, immo potius conformatur eidem et amminiculatur ad rerum productionem in esse. Similiter dicimus de partibus temporis. Ad instar naturalis huius iustitie animaduertit Plato rem publicam, que regitur iustitia positiua, esse informandam, ut, si quis in re publica uel uiribus corporis uel fortune commodis aliis preemineret, dictante tamen iustitia pateretur se inferioribus adequari. Et ideo de iustitia naturali premisit tractatum, ut competentius descenderet ad tractandum de iustitia positiua, per quam regitur res publica." Anonymous Magister Artium, *Accessus Philosophorum*, in Claude Lafleur, *Quatre introductions à la philosophie au XIIIe siècle: Textes critiques et études historiques* (Montréal: Institut d'Études Médiévales; Paris: Vrin, 1988), 232–33.

35. Aristotle offers this series of definitions, namely, six, in *Metaphysics* Δ. 4, 1014b16–1015a19. Medieval authors knew this passage from the Latin version, which is critically edited in the series *Aristoteles Latinus*. Cf. *Aristoteles Latinus. XXV.2. Metaphysica. Lib. I–X, XII–XIV. Translatio Anonyma sive 'Media'*, edited by Gudrun Vuillemin-Diem (Leiden: Brill, 1976), 88–89, 19. Aristotle offers an account of the different meanings of *natura* also in the second book of his *Physics*, at 193a29–b21. Cf. *Aristoteles Latinus: VII.1 Fasciculus secundus: Physica. Translatio Vetus*, edited by Ferdinand Bossier and Jozef Brams (Leiden: Brill, 1990), $47^5$–$49^{12}$.

36. See on this Gianfranco Fioravanti, *"Philosophi* contro *legistae*: Un momento dell'autoaffermazione della filosofia nel Medioevo," in *Miscellanea Mediaevalia*, Band 26: *Was ist Philosophie im Mittelalter?*, edited by Jan A. Aertsen and Andreas Speer (Berlin: Walter de Gruyter, 1998), 421–27.

37. Boyle, "The Inter-Conciliar Period."

38. See in particular Jan A. Aertsen, *Medieval Philosophy and the Transcendentals: The Case of Thomas Aquinas* (Leiden: Brill, 1996); Jan A. Aertsen, *Medieval Philosophy as Transcendental Thought: From Philip the Chancellor (ca. 1225) to Francisco Suárez* (Leiden: Brill, 2012). For an evaluation of Aertsen's works, see Carlos Bazán, "Thomas d'Aquin et les transcendantaux: Retour sur un livre de Jan A. Aertsen," *Revue des Sciences philosophiques et théologiques* 84 (2000): 93–104; Olivier Boulnois, "Une synthèse sur l'histoire de la métaphysique médiévale," *Recherches de théologie et philosophie médiévales* 80 (2013): 467–80.

39. Particularly interesting is the study of *ius naturale* that is developed in commentary to the *Nicomachean Ethics* that appears deeply influenced by Aquinas's teaching on natural law. See on this Odon Lottin,

*Psychologie et morale aux XIIe et XIIIe*, vol. 4: *Problèmes de morale* (Gembloux: Duculot, 1954), 521–48.

40. See Eugenio Randi, *Il sovrano e l'orologio: Due immagini di Dio nel dibattito sulla «potentia Dei absoluta» fra XIII e XIV secolo* (Florence: La Nuova Italia, 1987); Luca Bianchi, *Il vescovo e i filosofi: La condanna parigina del 1277 e l'evoluzione dell'aristotelismo scolastico* (Bergamo: Lubrina, 1990); Eugenio Randi and Luca Bianchi, *Le verità dissonanti: Aristotele alla fine del Medioevo*, (Rome: Laterza, 1990). On the 1277 condemnation, see also Roland Hissette, *Enquête sur les 219 articles condamnés à Paris le 7 mars 1277* (Louvain: Publication Universitaire—Vander-Oyez, 1977).

41. See on this Sylvain Piron, "Le plan de l'évêque: Pour une critique interne de la condamnation du 7 mars 1277," *Recherches de théologie et philosophie médiévale* 78 (2011): 383–415.

42. See Paul Vignaux, "Nominalisme," in *Dictionnaire de théologie catholique*, vol. 11 (Paris: Letouzey et Ané, 1931), 717–84 ; Paul Vignaux, *Nominalisme au XIVe siècle* (Montreal: Institut d'Études Médiévales, 1948). See also Alain de Libera, *La querelle des universaux de Platon à la fin du Moyen Âge* (Paris: Seuil, 1996).

43. See in particular Marino Damiata, *Guglielmo d'Ockham, povertà e potere*, 2 vols. (Florence: Studi Francescani, 1979); Roberto Lambertini, *La povertà pensata: Evoluzione storica della definizione dell'identità minoritica da Bonaventura a Ockham* (Modena: Mucchi, 2000).

44. See Arthur Stephen McGrade, *The Political Thought of William of Ockham* (Cambridge: Cambridge University Press, 1974); Arthur Stephen McGrade, "Natural Law and Moral Omnipotence," in *The Cambridge Companion to Ockham*, edited by Paul Vincent Spade (Cambridge: Cambridge University Press, 1999), 273–301.

45. See on this point Jürgen Miethke, "Einleitung," in Wilhelm von Ockham, *De potestate papae et cleri, III.1 Dialogus, vol. I – Die Amtsvollmacht von Papst und Klerus, III.1 Dialogus, Band I. Lateinisch / Deutsch*, Übersetzt und eingeleitet von Jürgen Miethke (Freiburg: Herder, 2015), 15–79; Jürgen Miethke, "The Power of Rulers and Violent Resistence Against an Unlawful Rule in the Political Theory of William of Ockham," *Revista de ciencia política* 24 (2004): 209–26. A general and comprehensive analysis of Ockham's political and legal discourse in historical context is available in Jürgen Miethke, *De potestate papae: Die päpstliche Amtskompetenz im Widerstreit der politischen Theorie von Thomas von Aquin bis Wilhelm von Ockham* (Tübingen: Mohr Siebeck, 2000); Jürgen Miethke,

*Politiktheorie im Mittelalter: Von Thomas von Aquin bis Wilhelm von Ockham* (Tübingen: Mohr Siebeck, 2008).

46. Huguccio, *Summa decretorum*, Tom. I: *Distinctiones I–XX*, edited by Oldřich Přerovský (Vatican City: Biblioteca Apostolica Vaticana, 2006), 7–10: "Ius ergo naturale dicitur ratio, scilicet naturalis uis animi ex qua homo discernit inter bonum et malum, eligendo bonum et detestando malum. . . . Dicitur etiam secundo loco ius naturale iudicium rationis scilicet motus proueniens ex ratione directe uel non directe. . . . Item tertio modo dicitur ius naturale instinctus et ordo nature. . . . Item quarto dicitur ius naturale ius diuinum, sicilicet quia continetur in lege mosayca et euangelica. . . . Et nota quod hoc ius, quantum ad demonstrationem, dicunt quidam esse quintam acceptionem iuris naturalis, scilicet omne licitum est approbatum, ita quod nec precipitur nec prohibetur."

47. Thomas Aquinas, *Sententia libri Ethicorum*, V, lec. 12, in *Sancti Thomae de Aquino Opera Omnia*, Tom. XLVII: *Sententia libri Ethicorum*, cura et studio fratrum praedicatorum, 2 vols. (Rome: Ad Sanctae Sabinae, 1969), 1:305[59–75]: "Est autem considerandum, quod iustum naturale est ad quod hominem natura inclinat. Attenditur autem in homine duplex natura. Una quidem, secundum quod est animal, quae est sibi aliisque animalibus communis; alia autem est natura hominis quae est propria sibi inquantum est homo, prout scilicet secundum rationem discernit turpe et honestum. Iuristae autem illud tantum dicunt ius naturale, quod consequitur inclinationem naturae communis homini et aliis animalibus, sicut coniunctio maris et feminae, educatio natorum, et alia huiusmodi. Illud autem ius, quod consequitur propriam inclinationem naturae humanae, inquantum scilicet homo est rationale animal, vocant ius gentium, quia eo omnes gentes utuntur, sicut quod pacta sint servanda, quod legati etiam apud hostes sint tuti, et alia huiusmodi. Utrumque autem horum comprehenditur sub iusto naturali, prout hic a philosopho accipitur."

48. Scattola, "Models in History of Natural Law."

49. Brian Tierney, *Liberty and Law: The Idea of Permissive Natural Law, 1100–1800* (Washington, DC: Catholic University of America Press, 2014).

## Conclusion

1. See on this the essays collected by Jason Taliadoros and Constant Mews in the *Journal of Religious History* 37.4 (2013): 435–527, especially

the following: Constant J. Mews, "Law, Theology, and Praxis, ca. 1140–1380: New Approaches to the Study of Law and Theology in Medieval Europe," 435–40; Claire Monagle, "Theology, Practice, and Policy at the Turn of the Thirteenth Century: the Papacy and Peter Lombard," 441–56; Atria A. Larson, "The Reception of Gratian's *Tractatus de poenitentia* and the Relationship between Canon Law and Theology in the Second Half of the Twelfth Century," 457–73; Jason Taliadoros, "Law, Theology, and Morality: Conceptions of the Rights to Relief of the Poor in the Twelfth and Thirteenth Centuries," 474–93; Tomas Zahora, "Attendant to a Higher Judge: Competing Paradigms of Legal Practice in the Thought of Alexander Neckam (1157–1217)," 494–509; Jasonne M. Grabher, "Making Practicality a Virtue: Morality, Law, and Fortitude in Giovanni da Legnano's *De Bello*," 510–27.

2. On the "long twelfth century" and the "renaissance of the twelfth century" there is a vast literature that begins with Charles Homer Haskins, *The Renaissance of the Twelfth Century* (Cambridge, MA: Harvard University Press, 1927). Important volumes on this new perspective concerning the twelfth century are Robert L. Benson and Giles Constable, eds., *Renaissance and Renewal in the Twelfth Century* (Cambridge, MA: Harvard University Press, 1982); Giles Constable, *The Reformation of the Twelfth Century* (Cambridge: Cambridge University Press, 1997); Robert Moore, *The First European Revolution* (Oxford: Oxford University Press, 2000). See also the recent collection, Thomas F. X. Noble and John Van Engen, eds., *European Transformations: The Long Twelfth Century* (Notre Dame, IN: University of Notre Dame Press, 2012).

3. See Piero Morpurgo, *L'armonia della natura e l'ordine dei governi (secoli XII–XIV)* (Florence: SISMEL – Edizioni del Galluzzo, 2000).

4. The implication of this perspective is the assumption that "nature" is the source of the moral order. On the complex evolution of this perspective in medieval discourse and on its pluralism, see Maaike van der Lugt, ed., *La nature comme source de la morale au Moyen Âge* (Florence: SISMEL—Edizioni del Galluzzo, 2014). A comprehensive analysis of the role of canon law and canonists in the construction of the European legal framework is offered in Orazio Condorelli, Franck Roumy, and Mathias Schmoeckel, eds., *Die Einfluss der Kanonistik auf die europäische Rechtskultur*, 4 vols. (Cologne: Böhlau, 2009–14).

5. See Francis Oakley, *Natural Law, Law of Nature, Natural Right: Continuity and Discontinuity in the History of Ideas* (New York: Continuum, 2005), 51–52.

6. Useful examples of this perspective are Berman's analysis of the rising of the plurality of juridical order and Yves Congar's evaluation of the connections between the ecclesiological debates at Paris since 1230 and the rise of a new historical order in European society. Berman, *Law and Revolution*; Yves Congar, "Aspects ecclésiologiques de la querelle entre mendiants et séculiers dans la seconde moitié du XIIIe siècle et le début du XIVe," *Archives d'histoire doctrinal et littéraire du Moyen Âge* 28 (1961): 35–151.

7. On the relevance of the "epistemological revolution" in the legal discourse in the fifteenth and sixteenth centuries, see Mathias Schmoeckel, *Das Rechts der Reformation: Die epistemologische Revolution der Wissenschaft und die Spaltung der Rechtsordnung in der Frühen Neuzeit* (Tübingen: Moher Siebeck, 2014).

8. See Brian Tierney, *Foundations of the Conciliar Theory: The Contribution of the Medieval Canonists from Gratian to the Great Schism* (Cambridge: Cambridge University Press, 1955); Brian Tierney, *Origins of Papal Infallibility, 1150–1350: A Study of the Concepts of Infallibility, Sovereignty and Tradition in the Middle Ages*, Second impression with a postscript (Leiden: Brill, 1988).

9. On the complex history of this principle, see Yves Congar, "Quod omnes tangit ab omnibus tractari et approbari debet," *Revue d'histoire du droit français et étranger* 36 (1958): 210–59, reprinted in Yves Congar, *Droit canon et structures ecclésiales* (London: Variorum, 1982); Costantin Fasolt, "*Quod omnes tangit ab omnibus approbari debet:* The Words and the Meaning," in *In Iure Veritas: Studies in Canon Law in Memory of Schafer Williams*, edited by Steven B. Brown and Blanche E. Cody (Cincinnati, OH: University of Cincinnati College of Law, 1991), 21–55; Andrea Bettini, "Riflessioni storico-dogmatiche sulla regola *quod omnes tangit* e la *persona ficta*," *Il diritto ecclesiastico* 3 (1999): 645–79; Jasmin Hauck, "*Quod omnes tangit debet ab omnibus approbari:* Eine Rechtsregel im Dialog der beiden Rechte," *Zeitschrift der Savigny-Stiftung für Rechtsgeschichte: Kanonistische Abteilung* 130 (2013): 398–417.

10. *Paradiso* 10.104–5.

# BIBLIOGRAPHY

PRIMARY SOURCES

Accursius. *Glossa ordinaria. See* Weigand, Rudolf.

Abelard, Peter. *Collationes.* Edited by John Marenbon and Giovanni Orlandi. Oxford: Oxford University Press, 2001.

———. *Ethica.* In *Petri Abaelardi Opera Theologica, IV: Scito te ipsum,* edited by Rainer M. Ilgner. Turnhout: Brepols, 2001.

Anonymous Magister Artium. *Accessus philosophorum.* In Claude Lafleur, *Quatre introductions à la philosophie au XIIIe siècle: Textes critiques et études historiques.* Montreal: Vrin; Paris: Institut d'Études médiévales, 1988.

Aquinas, Thomas. *Sententia libri Ethicorum.* In *Sancti Thomae de Aquino Opera Omnia,* Tom. XLVII: *Sententia libri Ethicorum,* cura et studio fratrum praedicatorum. 2 vols. Rome: Ad Sanctae Sabinae, 1969.

———. *Summa theologiae.* In *Sancti Thomae de Aquino Opera Omnia,* Tom. IV–XI: *Summa theologiae.* Cura et studio fratrum praedicatorum. 9 vols. Rome: Ad Sanctae Sabinae, 1888–1906.

Aristotle. *Metaphysics.* In *Aristoteles Latinus,* XXV.2 *Metaphysica Lib. I–x, XII–XIV. Translation Anonyma sive "Media."* Edited by Gudrun Vuillemin-Diem. Leiden: Brill, 1976.

———. *Physics.* In *Aristoteles Latinus,* VII.1. *Fasciculus secundus: Physica. Translatio Vetus.* Edited by Ferdinand Bossier and Jozef Brams. Leiden: Brill, 1990.

*Biblia Latina cum glossa ordinaria.* Edited by Adolph Rusch. 4 vols. Strassburg, 1480/81. Reprint. Turnhout: Brepols, 1992.

Dante Alighieri. *Commedia.* Edited by Anna Maria Chiavacci Leonardi. 3 vols. Milan: Arnoldo Mondadori, 2006. English translation in *The Divine Comedy by Dante Alighieri,* edited and translated by Robert M. Durling. 3 vols. New York: Oxford University Press, 1996.

———. *Rime.* In *Opere,* vol. 1: *Rime, Vita Nova, De Vulgari Eloquentia,* edited by Claudio Giunta, Guglielmo Gorni, Mirko Tavoni, with introduction by Marco Santagata. Milan: Arnoldo Mondadori, 2011. English translation *Dante's Rime*, translated by Patrick S. Diehl. Princeton, NJ: Princeton University Press, 1979.

*The Digest of Justinian.* Edited by Charles Henry Monro and William Warwick Buckland. Cambridge: Cambridge University Press, 1904.

Duns Scotus, John. *Quaestiones in Libros I–IV Sententiarum.* In *Joannis Duns Scoti Opera Omnia*, vols. V–X. Lyon, 1639. Reprint. Hildesheim: Olms, 1968.

Gerson, Jean. *Definitiones terminorum theologiae moralis.* In *Oeuvres complètes*, vol. 9, edited by Palémon Glorieux, 133–42. Paris: Desclée, 1973.

———. *De vita spirituali animae.* In *Oeuvres complètes*, vol. 3, edited by Palémon Glorieux, 113–202. Paris: Desclée, 1962.

Gratian. *Concordia discordantium canonum (Decretum).* In *Corpus Iuris Canonici*, 2 vols., edited by Emil Friedberg, vol. 1. Leipzig: B. Tauchnitz, 1879.

*Gratian: The Treatise on Laws (Decrectum DD. 1–20).* Translated by Augustine Thompson, *with the Ordinary Gloss*, translated by James Gordley, with introduction by Katherine Christensen. Washington, DC: Catholic University of America Press, 1993.

Guarnerius Iurisprudentissimus. *Liber divinarum sententiarum.* Edited by Giuseppe Mazzanti. Spoleto: Centro Italiano di studi sull'Alto Medioevo, 1999.

Huguccio. *Summa decretorum*, Tom. I: *Distinctiones I–XX*. Edited by Oldřich Přerovský. Vatican City: Biblioteca Apostolica Vaticana, 2006.

*Iohannis Scoti seu Eriugenae Periphyseon: Liber Primus.* Edited by Édouard Jeauneau. Turnhout: Brepols, 1996.

Locke, John. *Two Treatises of Government: A Critical Edition by Peter Laslett.* Cambridge: Cambridge University Press, 1960.

Ockham, William. *Quodlibeta Septem.* In *Guillelmi de Ochkam Opera Philosophica et Theologica: Opera Theologica, IX*, edited by Institutus Franciscanus Universitatis S. Bonaventurae. New York: St. Bonaventure University, 1980.

Stephen of Tournai (Stephanus Tornacensis). *Die Summa über das Decretum Gratiani.* Edited by Johann F. von Schulte. Giessen: Emil Roth, 1891.

SECONDARY SOURCES

Aertsen, Jan A. *Medieval Philosophy and the Transcendentals: The Case of Thomas Aquinas*. Leiden: Brill, 1996.

———. *Medieval Philosophy as Transcendental Thought: From Philip the Chancellor (ca. 1225) to Francisco Suárez*. Leiden: Brill, 2012.

Bastit, Michel. *Naissance de la loi moderne*. Paris: Presses Universitaires de France, 1990.

Bazán, Carlos. "Thomas d'Aquin et les transcendentaux: Retour sur un livre de Jan A. Aertsen." *Revue des Sciences philosophiques et théologiques* 84 (2002): 93–104.

Bender, Peter. *Die Rezeption des römischen Rechts im Urteil der deutschen Rechtswissenschaft*. Frankfurt am Main: Lang, 1979.

Benson, Robert L., and Giles Constable, eds. *Renaissance and Renewal in the Twelfth Century*. Cambridge, MA: Harvard University Press, 1982.

Berlin, Isaiah. "Two Concepts of Liberty." In *Four Essays on Liberty*. Oxford: Oxford University Press, 1969.

Berman, Harold. *Law and Revolution: The Formation of the Western Legal Tradition*. Cambridge, MA: Harvard University Press, 1983.

Besta, Enrico. *L'opera d'Irnerio (Contributo alla storia del diritto Italiano)*. Turin: Arnaldo Forni Editori, 1896.

Bettetini, Andrea. "Riflessioni storico-dogmatiche sulla regola *quod omnes tangit* e la *persona ficta*." *Il diritto ecclesiastico* 3 (1999): 645–79.

Bianchi, Luca. *Il vescovo e i filosofi: La condanna parigina del 1277 e l'evoluzione dell'aristotelismo scolastico*. Bergamo: Lubrina, 1990.

Black, Rufus. "Introduction: The New Natural Law Theory." In *The Revival of Natural Law: Philosophical, Theological and Ethical Responses to the Finnis-Grisez School*, edited by Nigel Biggar and Rufus Black, 1–25. Aldershot: Ashgate, 2000.

———. "Is the New Natural Law Theory Christian?" In *The Revival of Natural Law: Philosophical, Theological and Ethical Responses to the Finnis-Grisez School*, edited by Nigel Biggar and Rufus Black, 148–62. Aldershot: Ashgate, 2000.

Blumenberg, Hans. *Die Legitimität der Neuzeit*. 2nd ed. Frankfurt am Main: Suhrkamp Verlag, 1974.

Bodenheimer, Edgar. "The Natural-Law Doctrine before the Tribunal of Science: A Reply to Hans Kelsen." *Western Political Quarterly* 3 (1950): 335–63.

Bolaffi, Angelo. *Il crepuscolo della sovranità: Filosofia e politica nella Germania del Novecento.* Rome: Donzelli, 2002.

Boulnois, Olivier. "Une synthèse sur l'histoire de la métaphysique médiévale." *Recherches de théologie et philosophie médiévales* 80 (2013): 467–80.

Boyle, Leonard E. "The Inter-conciliar Period: 1179–1215 and the Beginnings of Pastoral Manuals." In *Miscellanea Rolando Bandinelli, Papa Alessandro III*, edited by Filippo Liotta, 43–56. Siena: Accademia Senese degli Intronati, 1986.

Brett, Annabel. *Liberty, Right and Nature: Individual Rights in Later Scholastic Thought.* Cambridge: Cambridge University Press, 1997.

———. "Scholastic Political Thought and the Modern Concept of the State." In *Rethinking the Foundations of Modern Political Thought*, edited by James Tully and Annabel Brett, 130–48. Cambridge: Cambridge University Press, 2006.

Brunner, Otto, Werner Conze, and Reinhart Koselleck, eds. *Geschichtliche Grundbegriffe: Historisches Lexikon zur politisch-sozialen Sprache in Deutschland.* 8 vols. Stuttgart: Klett-Cotta, 1972–97.

Burns, James H., ed. *The Cambridge History of Medieval Political Thought, c. 350–c. 1450.* Cambridge: Cambridge University Press, 2008.

Calasso, Francesco. *I glossatori e la teoria della sovranità: Studio di diritto comune pubblico.* Milan: Giuffrè Editore, 1951.

———. *Medio evo del diritto: I–Le fonti.* Milan: Giuffrè Editore, 1954.

Carlyle, Robert Warraud, and Alexander James Carlyle. *A History of the Mediaeval Political Theory in the West*, vol. 5: *The Political Theory of the Thirteenth Century.* Edinburgh: William Blackwood & Sons, 1903.

Chappell, Timothy. "Natural Law Revived: Natural Law Theory and Contemporary Moral Philosophy." In *The Revival of Natural Law: Philosophical, Theological and Ethical Responses to the Finnis-Grisez School*, edited by Nigel Biggar and Rufus Black, 29–52. Aldershot: Ashgate, 2000.

Chenu, Marie-Dominique. *Dimension nouvelle de la chrétienté.* Paris: Le Cerf, 1937.

———. "Review of Jacques Maritain, *Humanisme intégral.*" *Bulletin thomiste* 15 (1938): 360–64.

———. *La théologie comme science au XIIIème siècle.* Paris: Vrin, 1957.

———. *La théologie au XIIe siècle.* Paris: Vrin, 1976.

Chevalier, Jacques. *Histoire de la pensée*, vol. 2: *La pensée chrétienne.* Paris: Flammarion, 1956.

Cmiel, Kenneth. "The Recent History of Human Rights." *American Historical Review* 109 (2004): 117–35.

Colish, Marcia. *Medieval Foundations of the Western Intellectual Tradition, 400–1400.* New Haven, CT: Yale University Press, 1998.

Condorelli, Orazio, Franck Roumy, and Mathias Schmoeckel, eds. *Die Einfluss der Kanonistik auf die europäische Rechtskultur.* 4 vols. Cologne: Böhlau, 2009–14.

Congar, Yves. "Aspects ecclésiologiques de la querelle entre mendiants et séculiers dans la seconde moitié du XIIIe siècle et le début du XIVe." *Archives d'histoire doctrinale et littéraire du Moyen Âge* 28 (1961): 35–151.

———. "Quod omnes tangit ab omnibus tractari et approbari debet." *Revue d'histoire du droit français et étranger* 36 (1958): 210–59. Reprinted in Yves Congar, *Droit canon et structures ecclésiales.* London: Variorum, 1982

Constable, Giles. *The Reformation of the Twelfth Century.* Cambridge: Cambridge University Press, 1997.

Conte, Emanuele. "Droit médiéval: Un débat historiographique italien," *Annales. Histoire. Sciences Sociales* 57 (2002): 1593–1613.

———. "Storia interna e storia esterna: Il diritto medievale da Francesco Calasso alla fine del XX secolo." *Rivista internazionale di diritto comune* 17 (2006): 299–322.

Cortese, Ennio. *La norma giuridica: Spunti teorici nel diritto comune classico.* 2 vols. Milan: Giuffrè Editore, 1962–64.

Courtney Murray, John. *We Hold These Truths: Catholic Reflections on the American Proposition.* Kansas City: Sheed & Ward, 1960.

Damiata, Marino. *Guglielmo d'Ockham, povertà e potere.* 2 vols. Florence: Studi Francescani, 1979.

De Ghellinck, Joseph. *Le mouvement théologique du XIIe siècle: Sa préparation lointaine avant et autour de Pierre Lombard ses rapports avec les initiatives des canonistes. Études, recherches et documents.* Bruges: Ed. Du Temple, 1948.

de Lagarde, Georges. *La naissance de l'esprit laïque au déclin du Moyen Âge.* Vol. 6: *L'individualisme Ockhamiste: La morale et le droit.* Paris: Presses Universitaires de France, 1946.

De Libera, Alain. *La querelle des universaux de Platon à la fin du Moyen Âge.* Paris: Seuil, 1996.

Delhaye, Philippe. *La philosophie chrétienne au Moyen Âge.* Paris: Fayard, 1959.

der Lugt, Maaike van, ed. *La nature comme source de la morale au Moyen Âge.* Florence: SISMEL—Edizioni del Galluzzo, 2014.

Diggins, John Patrick. "Arthur O. Lovejoy and the Challenge of Intellectual History." *Journal of the History of Ideas* 67 (2006): 181–208.

Dilcher, Gerhard. "Genossenschaftstheorie und Sozialrecht: ein Juristensozialismus Otto von Gierkes?" *Quaderni fiorentini* 3–4 (1974–75): 319–65.

Errera, Andrea. *Arbor actionum: Genere letterario e forma di classificazione delle azioni nella dottrina dei glossatori.* Bologna: Monduzzi, 1995.

———. *Lineamenti di epistemologia giuridica medievale: Storia di una rivoluzione scientifica.* Turin: Giappichelli, 2006.

Fantappiè, Carlo. *Chiesa romana e modernità giuridica*, vol. 1: *L'Edificazione del sistema canonistico (1563–1903).* Milan: Giuffrè Editore, 2008.

———. *Chiesa romana e modernità giuridica*, vol. 2: *Il Codex iuris canonici (1917).* Milan: Giuffrè Editore, 2008.

———. "Diritto canonico codificato." In *Dizionario del sapere storico-religioso del '900*, edited by Alberto Melloni, 654–700. Bologna: Il Mulino, 2010.

Fantini, Maria Grazia. *La cultura del giurista medievale: Natura, causa, ratio.* Rome: Franco Angeli, 1998.

Fasolt, Constantine. "*Quod omnes tangit ab omnibus approbari debet :* The Words and the Meaning." In *In Iure Veritas: Studies in Canon Law in Memory of Schafer Williams*, edited by Steven B. Brown and Blanche E. Cody, 21–55. Cincinnati, OH: University of Cincinnati College of Law, 1991.

Feci, Simona. "Mazzolini Silvestro (Silvestro da Prierio, Prierias, Prieriate)." In *Dizionario Biografico degli Italiani*, 72:678–81. Rome: Istituto dell'Enciclopedia Italiana, 2009.

Figgis, John Neville. *Political Thought from Gerson to Grotius, 1414–1625: Seven Studies.* Cambridge: Cambridge University Press, 1907; New York: Harper & Brothers, 1960.

———. "Review of *A History of Medieval Political Theory in the West.*" *English Historical Review* 19 (1904): 330–33; 25 (1910): 561–64; 31 (1916): 305–6.

Fimister, Alan Paul. *Robert Schuman: Neo-Scholastic Humanism and the Reunification of Europe*. Brussels: Peter Lang, 2008.

Finnis, John. *Aquinas: Moral, Political, and Legal Theory*. Oxford: Oxford University Press, 1998.

——. "Aquinas on *ius* and Hart on Rights: A Response to Tierney." *Review of Politics* 64 (2002): 407–10.

——. *Natural Law and Natural Rights*. 2nd ed. Oxford: Oxford University Press, [1980] 2011.

——. "Natural Law Theories." In *Stanford Encyclopedia of Philosophy*. Stanford, CA: Center for the Study of Language and Information, 2011. http://plato.stanford.edu/archives/fall2011/entries/natural-law-theories/.

Fioravanti, Gianfranco. "*Philosophi* contro *legistae*: Un momento dell'autoaffermazione della filosofia nel Medioevo." In *Miscellanea Mediaevalia*, Band 26: *Was ist Philosophie im Mittelalter?*, edited by Jan A. Aertsen and Andreas Speer, 421–27. Berlin: Walter de Gruyter, 1998.

Flores, Marcello. *Storia dei diritti umani*. Bologna: Il Mulino, 2008.

Forest, Aime, Ferdinand Van Steenberghen, and Maurice de Gandillac, eds. *Le mouvement doctrinal du XIème au XIVème siècle*. Paris: Bloud & Gay, 1956.

Fuchs, Maximilian. "La 'Genossenschaftstheorie' di Otto von Gierke come fonte primaria della teoria generale del diritto di Santi Romano." *Materiali per una storia della cultura giuridica* 9 (1979): 65–80.

Fusaro, Diego. *L'orizzonte in movimento: Modernità e futuro in Reinhardt Koselleck*. Bologna: Il Mulino, 2012.

Ganger, Sten. "Vorbemerkung zum Thema 'Dominium' bei Ockham." *Miscellanea mediaevalia* 9 (1974): 293–327.

Gemelli, Agostino. "Leggende e pregiudizi in tema di Scolastica." *Rivista di filosofia neoscolastica* 7 (1915): 3–27.

——. "Medievalismo." *Vita e Pensiero* 1 (1914): 1–24. Reprinted in *Idee e battaglie per la cultura cattolica*, 3–33. Milan: Società editrice "Vita e Pensiero," 1931.

Gierke, Otto von. *Das deutsche Genossenschaftsrecht*. 4 vols. Berlin: Weidmann, 1868–1913.

——. *Natural Law and the Theory of Society, 1500 to 1800: With a Lecture on the Ideas of Natural Law and Humanity by Ernst Troeltch*. Translated with an introduction by Ernest Barker. Cambridge: Cambridge University Press, 1934; Boston: Beacon Press, 1957.

————. *Political Theories of the Middle Ages.* Translated with an introduction by Frederic William Maitland. Cambridge: Cambridge University Press, 1900.

Gilson, Étienne. *Introduction à l'étude de Saint Augustin.* Paris: Vrin, 1927.

————. *La philosophie au Moyen Âge.* Paris: Payot, 1962.

————. *L'esprit de la philosophie médiéval.* Paris: Vrin, [1932] 1969.

Giraud, Cédric. *Per verba magistri: Anselme de Laon et son école au XIIe siècle.* Turnhout: Brepols, 2010.

Grabher, Jasonne M. "Making Practicality a Virtue: Morality, Law, and Fortitude in Giovanni da Legnano's *De Bello.*" *Journal of Religious History* 37 (2013): 510–27.

Grabmann, Martin. *Die Geschichte der katholischen Theologie seit dem Ausgang der Väterzeit.* Freiburg im Breigau: Herder, 1933.

————. *Die Geschichte der scholastischen Methode.* 2 vols. Freiburg: Herder, 1909–11.

————. "Das Naturrecht der Scholastik von Gratian bis Thomas von Aquin." *Archiv für Rechtsphilosophie* 26 (1922): 12–53. Reprinted in *Mittelalterliches Geistesleben: Abhandlungen zur Geschichte der Scholastik und Mystik,* 65–103. Munich: Max Huber Verlag, 1926.

Gregory, Tullio. *Speculum naturale: Percorsi del pensiero medievale.* Rome: Edizioni di Storia e Letteratura, 2007.

Grisez, Germain G. "The First Principle of Practical Reason: A Commentary on the *Summa Theologiae,* 1–2, Question 94, Article 2." *Natural Law Forum* 10 (1965): 168–201.

Grossi, Paolo. *L'ordine giuridico medievale.* New ed. Rome: Laterza, 2011.

Gualazzini, Ugo. "Natura id est Deus." *Studia Gratiana* 3 (1955): 413–24.

Hart, Herbert Lionel A. "Are There Any Natural Rights?" *Philosophical Review* 64 (1955): 175–91.

Haskins, Charles Homer. *The Renaissance of the Twelfth Century.* Cambridge, MA: Harvard University Press, 1927.

Hauck, Jasmin. "*Quod omnes tangit debet ab omnibus approbari:* Eine Rechtsregel im Dialog der beiden Rechte." *Zeitschrift der Savigny-Stiftung für Rechtsgeschichte. Kanonistische Abteilung* 130 (2013): 398–417.

Hissette, Roland. *Enquête sur les 219 articles condamnés à Paris le 7 mars 1277.* Louvain: Publication Universitaire—Vander-Oyez, 1977.

Höhn, Reinhard. *Otto von Gierke Staatslehre und unsere Zeit: Zugleich eine Auseinandersetzung mit dem Rechtssystem des 19. Jahrhunderts.* Hamburg: Hanseatische Verlagsanstalt, 1936.

Hollerbach, Alexander. "Das Verhältnis der katholischen Naturrechtslehre des 19. Jahrhunderts zur Geschichte der Rechtswissenschaft und Rechtsphilosophie." In *Theologie und Sozialethik im Spannungsfeld der Gesellschaft: Untersuchungen zur Ideengeschichte des deutschen Katholizismus im 19. Jahrhundert*, edited by Albrecht Langner, 113–33. Munich: Schöningh, 1974.

von Inwagen, Peter. "The Nature of Metaphysics." In *Contemporary Readings in the Foundation of Metaphysics*, edited by Stephen Laurence and Cynthia Macdonald, 11–21. Oxford: Blackwell, 1998.

Kelsen, Hans. *General Theory of Law and State*. Cambridge, MA: Harvard University Press, 1945.

———. "The Natural-Law Doctrine before the Tribunal of Science." *Western Political Quarterly* 2 (1949): 481–513.

Koselleck, Reinhart. "Historik und Hermeneutik." In *Kritik und Krise: Ein Beitrag zur Pathogenese der bürglichen Welt*. Freiburg: K. Alber, 1959.

———. *Zeitschichten: Studien zur Historik. Mit einem Beitrag von Hans-Georg Gadamer*. Frankfurt am Main: Suhrkamp Verlag, 2000.

Krupa, Hans. "Genossenschaftslehre und soziologischer Pluralismus: Ein Beitrag zur Staatslehre Otto von Gierkes." *Archiv des öffentlichen Rechts* 32 (1940–41): 97–114.

Kuttner, Stephan. "Gratian and Plato." In *Church and Government in the Middle Ages: Essays Presented to C. R. Cheney*, edited by Christopher N. L. Brooke et al., 93–118. Cambridge: Cambridge University Press, 1976. Reprinted in *History of Ideas and Doctrines of Canon Law in the Middle Ages*, XI. London: Variorum, 1980.

———. *Repertorium der Kanonistik (1140–1234): Prodromus Corporis glossarum*. Vatican City: Biblioteca Apostolica Vaticana, [1937] 1981.

Ilting, Karl-Heinz. "Naturrecht." In *Geschichtliche Grundbegriffe: Historisches Lexikon zur politisch-sozialen Sprache in Deutschland*, edited by Otto Brunner, Werner Conze, and Reinhart Koselleck, 4:245–313. Stuttgart: Klett-Cotta, 1972–97.

Lambertini, Roberto. *La povertà pensata: Evoluzione storica della definizione dell'identità monolitica da Bonaventura a Ockham*. Modena: Mucchi, 2000.

Larson, Atria A. "The Reception of Gratian's *Tractatus de penitentia* and the Relationship between Canon Law and Theology in the Second Half of the Twelfth Century." *Journal of Religious History* 37 (2013): 457–73.

Leff, Gordon. *Medieval Thought from St. Augustine to Ockham.* Harmondsworth: Middlesex, 1958.

Lewis, John P. *The Genossenschaft Theory of Otto von Gierke: A Study in Political Thought.* Madison: University of Wisconsin Press, 1935.

Lottin, Odon. "La définition classique de la loi: Commentaires historiques de la Ia IIae q. 90." *Revue néo-scholastique de philosophie* 27 (1925): 129–45, 243–73.

———. "Le droit naturel chez saint Thomas et ses prédécesseurs." *Ephemerides theologicae Lovanienses* 1 (1924): 369–88; 2 (1925): 32–53, 345–66; 3 (1926): 155–76.

———. *Le droit naturel chez saint Thomas d'Aquin et ses prédécesseurs.* Bruges: Ch. Beyaert, 1931.

———. "Le premiers exposés scolastiques sur la loi éternelle." *Ephemerides theologicae Lovanienses* 14 (1937): 287–301.

———. *Psychologie et morale aux XIIe et XIIIe siècles*, vol. 2: *Problèmes de morale.* Gembloux: Duculot, 1948.

———. *Psychologie et morale aux XIIe et XIIIe siècles*, vol. 4: *Problèmes de morale.* Gembloux: Duculot, 1954.

———. *Psychologie et morale aux XIIe et XIIIe siècles*, vol. 5: *Problèmes d'histoire littéraire: L'école d'Anselme de Laon et de Guillaume de Champeaux.* Gembloux: Duculot, 1957.

Lovejoy, Arthur O. *The Great Chain of Being: A Study of the History of an Idea.* Cambridge, MA: Harvard University Press, 1936.

———. "Reflections on the History of Ideas." *Journal of the History of Ideas* 1 (1940): 2–23.

Luscombe, David. *The School of Peter Abelard: The Influence of Abelard's Thought in the Early Scholastic Period.* Cambridge: Cambridge University Press, 1969.

MacCormick, Neil. *H. L. A. Hart.* London: Edward Arnold, 1981.

Maitland, Frederic William. "Translator's Introduction." In Otto von Gierke, *Political Theories of the Middle Ages*, translated with an introduction by Frederic William Maitland, vii–xlvi. Cambridge: Cambridge University Press, 1900.

Marenbon, John. "Abelard's Concept of Natural Law." In *Miscellanea Mediaevalia*, Band 21.2: *Mensch und Natur im Mittelalter*, edited by Albert Zimmermann, 609–21. Berlin: Walter de Gruyter, 1992.

Maritain, Jacques. *Humanisme intégral: Problèmes temporals et spirituels d'une nouvelle chrétienté.* Paris: Ferdinand Aubier, 1936.

————. "L'Idéal historique d'une nouvelle chrétienté." *La vie intellectuelle* (1935).

————. *Man and the State*. Washington, DC: Catholic University of America Press, 1952.

Martin, Rex, and James W. Nickel. "A Bibliography of the Nature and Foundations of Rights." *Political Theory* 6.3 (1978): 395–413.

Martinez, Peces-Barba. "Michel Villey et les droits de l'homme." *Droit et société* 71 (2009): 93–100.

McGrade, Stephen Arthur. "Natural Law and Moral Omnipotence." In *The Cambridge Companion to Ockham*, edited by Paul Vincent Spade, 273–301. Cambridge: Cambridge University Press, 1999.

————. *The Political Thought of William of Ockham*. Cambridge: Cambridge University Press, 1974.

McInerny, Ralph. "Grisez and Thomism." In *The Revival of Natural Law: Philosophical, Theological and Ethical Responses to the Finnis-Grisez School*, edited by Nigel Biggar and Rufus Black, 53–72. Aldershot: Ashgate, 2000.

Melloni, Alberto. "Diritto canonico." In *Dizionario del sapere storico-religioso del Novecento*, edited by Alberto Melloni, 647–53. Bologna: Il Mulino, 2010.

Menozzi, Daniele. "La chiesa e la storia: Una dimensione della cristianità da Leone XIII al Vaticano II." *Cristianesimo nella storia* 5 (1985): 69–106.

————. *Chiesa e diritti umani*. Bologna: Il Mulino, 2012.

Mews, Constant J. "Law, Theology, and Praxis ca. 1140–1380: New Approaches to the Study of Law and Theology in Medieval Europe." *Journal of Religious History* 37 (2013): 435–40.

Miethke, Jürgen. "Einleitung." In Wilhelm von Ockham, *De potestate papae et cleri, III.1 Dialogus, vol. I: Die Amtsvollmacht von Papst und Klerus, III.1 Dialogus, Band I: Lateinisch / Deutsch*, edited by Jürgen Miethke, 15–79. Freiburg: Herder, 2015.

————. *Politiktheorie im Mittelalter: Von Thomas von Aquin bis Wilhelm von Ockham*. Tübingen: Mohr Siebeck, 2008.

————. *De potestate papae: Die päpstliche Amtskompetenz im Widerstreit der politischen Theorie von Thomas von Aquin bis Wilhelm von Ockham*. Tübingen: Mohr Siebeck, 2000.

————. "The Power of Rulers and Violent Resistence against an Unlawful Rule in the Political Theory of William of Ockham." *Revista de ciencia política* 24 (2004): 209–26.

Monagle, Claire. "Theology, Practice, and Policy at the Turn of the Thirteenth Century: The Papacy and Peter Lombard." *Journal of Religious History* 37 (2013): 441–56.

Moore, Robert. *The First European Revolution*. Oxford: Oxford University Press, 2000.

Morpurgo, Piero. *L'armonia della natura e l'ordine dei governi (secoli XII–XIV)*. Florence: SISMEL—Edizioni del Galluzzo, 2000.

Morris, Colin. *The Discovery of the Individual, 1050–1200*. London: SPCK, 1972.

Nederman, Cary. "Conciliarism and Constitutionalism: Jean Gerson and Medieval Political Thought." *History of European Ideas* 12 (1990): 189–200.

———. "Constitutionalism—Medieval and Modern: Against Neo-Figgiste Orthodoxy (Again)." *History of Political Thought* 17 (1996): 179–94.

———. "Empire and the Historiography of European Political Thought: Marsiglio of Padua, Nicholas of Cusa, and the Medieval–Modern Divide." *Journal of the History of Ideas* 66 (2005): 1–15.

———. "Introduction to the Transaction Edition." In Alessandro Passerin d'Entrèves, *Natural Law: An Introduction to Legal Philosophy*, i–xiv. 1951; New Brunswick, NJ: Transaction Publishers, 1994.

———. "Review of Brian Tierney, *The Idea of Natural Rights: Studies on Natural Rights, Natural Law, and Church Law, 1150–1625*, and *Rights, Law, and Infallibility in Medieval Thought*." *American Journal of Legal History* 42 (1998): 217–19.

Noble, Thomas F. X., and John Van Engen, eds. *European Transformations: The Long Twelfth Century*. Notre Dame, IN: University of Notre Dame Press, 2012.

Northcott, Michael. "The Moral Standing of Nature and the New Natural Law." In *The Revival of Natural Law: Philosophical, Theological and Ethical Responses to the Finnis-Grisez School*, edited by Nigel Biggar and Rufus Black, 262–81. Aldershot: Ashgate, 2000.

Oakley, Francis. *The Conciliarist Tradition: Constitutionalism in the Catholic Church, 1300–1870*. Oxford: Oxford University Press, 2003.

———. "Figgis, Constance, and the Divines of Paris." *American Historical Review* 75 (1969): 368–86.

———. "Gerson and d'Ailly: An Admonition." *Speculum* 40 (1965): 74–83. Reprinted in *Natural Law, Conciliarism and Consent in the Late Middle Ages*, chap. 5. London: Variorum, 1984.

————. "Lovejoy's Unexpected Option." *Journal of the History of Ideas* 48 (1987): 231–45.

————. "Medieval Theories of Natural Law: William of Ockham and the Significance of the Voluntarist Tradition." *Natural Law Forum* 6 (1961): 65–83. Reprinted in *Natural Law, Conciliarism, and Consent in the Late Middle Ages*, chap. 15. London: Variorum, 1984.

————. "Natural Law, the Corpus Mysticum, and Consent in Conciliar Thought from John of Paris to Matthias Ugonis." *Speculum* 56 (1981): 786–810.

————. *Natural Law, Law of Nature, Natural Rights: Continuity and Discontinuity in the History of Ideas*. New York: Continuum, 2005.

————. "Pierre d'Ailly." In *Reformers in Profile: Advocates of Reform, 1300–1600*, edited by Brian A. Gerrish, 40–57. Philadelphia, PA: Fortress Press, 1967. Reprinted in *Natural Law, Conciliarism, and Consent in the Late Middle Ages*, chap. 2. London: Variorum, 1984.

————. "Pierre d'Ailly and the Absolute Power of God: Another Note on the Theology of Nominalism," *Harvard Theological Review* 56 (1963): 59–73. Reprinted in *Natural Law, Conciliarism, and Consent in the Late Middle Ages*, chap. 3. London: Variorum, 1984.

————. *The Political Thought of Pierre d'Ailly: The Voluntarist Tradition*. New Haven, CT: Yale University Press, 1964.

————. *Politics and Eternity: Studies in the History of Medieval and Early-Modern Political Thought*. Leiden: Brill, 1999.

Padovani, Andrea. *Perché chiedi il mio nome? Dio natura e diritto nel secolo XII*. Turin: Giappichelli Editore, 1997.

Patti, M. *Chiesa cattolica tedesca e Terzo Reich (1933–1945)*. Brescia: Morcelliana, 2008.

Passerin d'Entrèves, Alessandro. *La filosofia politica medievale: Appunti di storia delle dottrine politiche*. Turin: Giappichelli, 1934.

————. *Medieval Contribution to Political Thought: Thomas Aquinas, Marsilius of Padua, Richard Hooker*. New York: Humanities Press, 1959.

————. *Natural Law: An Introduction to Legal Philosophy*. New York: Hutchinson's University Library, 1951; New Brunswick, NJ: Transaction Publishers, 1994.

Pennington, Kenneth. "The *Big Bang*: Roman Law in the Early Twelfth Century." *Rivista internazionale di diritto comune* 18 (2007): 43–70.

————. "*Lex naturalis* and *Ius naturale.*" *Jurist* 68 (2008): 569–91. Reprinted in *Crossing Boundaries at Medieval Universities*, edited by Spencer E. Young, 227–53. Leiden: Brill, 2011.

————. *The Prince and the Law, 1200–1600: Sovereignty and Rights in the Western Legal Tradition.* Berkeley: University of California Press, 1993.

Pfeiffer-Munz, Susanne. *Soziales Recht ist deutsches Recht: Otto von Gierkes Theorie des sozialen Rechts untersucht anhand seiner Stellungnahmen zur deutschen und zur schweizerischen Privatrechtskodifikation.* Zurich: Schulthess, 1979.

Piron, Sylvain. "Le plan de l'évêque. Pour une critique interne de la condamnation du 7 mars 1277." *Recherches de théologie et philosophie médiévale* 78 (2011): 383–415.

Pocock, John. *Barbarism and Religion.* Vol. 3: *The First Decline and Fall.* Cambridge: Cambridge University Press, 2003.

————. *The Machiavellian Moment: Florentine Political Thought and the Atlantic Republican Tradition.* Princeton, NJ: Princeton University Press, 1975.

Prodi, Paolo. *Una storia della giustizia: Dal pluralismo dei fori al moderno dualismo tra coscienza e diritto.* Bologna: Il Mulino, 2000.

Quaglioni, Diego. *La giustizia nel Medioevo e nella prima età moderna.* Bologna: Il Mulino, 2004.

Randi, Eugenio. *Il sovrano e l'orologio: Due immagini di Dio nel dibattito sulla «potentia Dei absoluta» fra XIII e XIV secolo.* Florence: La Nuova Italia, 1987.

Randi Eugenio, and Luca Bianchi. *Le verità dissonanti: Aristotele alla fine del Medioevo.* Rome: Laterza, 1990.

Ried, Charles. "The Medieval Origins of the Western Natural Rights Tradition: The Achievement of Brian Tierney." *Cornell Law Review* 83 (1998): 437–63.

Rommen, Heinrich. *Die ewige Wiederkehr des Naturrechts.* Leipzig: Jakob Hegner, 1936. English version *The Natural Law: A Study in Legal and Social History and Philosophy*, translated by Thomas R. Hanley. Washington, DC: Herder Book Co., 1947. 2nd ed., edited by Russell Hittinger. Indianapolis, IN: Liberty Fund, 1998.

Scattola, Merio. "Models in History of Natural Law." *Ius commune: Zeitschrift für Europäische Rechtsgeschichte* 28 (2001): 91–159.

————. "Storia dei concetti e storia delle discipline politiche." *Storia della storiografia* 49 (2006): 95–124.

Schmoeckel, Mathias. *Das Rechts der Reformation: Die epistemologische Revolution der Wissenschaft und die Spaltung der Rechtsordnung in der Frühen Neuzeit.* Tübingen: Mohr Siebeck, 2004.

Schouppe, Jean-Pierre. "Reflexions sur la conception du droit de M. Villey: Une alternative à son rejet des droits de l'homme." *Persona y derecho* 25 (1991): 151–69.

Seagrave, Adam S. "How Old Are Modern Rights? On the Lockean Roots of Contemporary Human Rights Discourse." *Journal of the History of Ideas* 72 (2011): 305–27.

———. "Identity and Diversity in the History of Ideas: A Reply to Brian Tierney." *Journal of the History of Ideas* 73 (2012): 163–66.

Shestack, Jerome J. "The Philosophical Foundations of Human Rights." *Human Rights Quarterly* 20.2 (1998): 201–34.

Simon, Yves R. *Philosophy of Democratic Government.* Chicago: University of Chicago Press, 1951.

Skinner, Quentin. *The Foundations of Modern Political Thought.* Vol. 1. Cambridge: Cambridge University Press, 1978.

Southern, Richard W. *Scholastic Humanism and the Unification of Europe.* 2 vols. Oxford: Blackwell, 1995–2001.

Steinberg, John P. *Dante and the Limits of the Law.* Chicago: University of Chicago Press, 2014.

Strauss, Leo. *Natural Right and History.* Chicago: University of Chicago Press, 1953.

Taliadoros, Jason. "Law, Theology, and Morality: Conceptions of the Rights to Relief of the Poor in the Twelfth and Thirteenth Centuries." *Journal of Religious History* 37 (2013): 474–93.

Tierney, Brian. "Conciliarism, Corporatism, and Individualism: The Doctrine of Subjective Rights in Gerson." *Cristianesimo nella storia* 9 (1988): 81–110.

———. "Corporatism, Individualism, and Consent: Locke and Premodern Thought." In *Law as Profession and Practice in Medieval Europe: Essays in Honor of James Brundage,* edited by Kenneth Pennington and Melodie H. Eichbauer, 49–71. Farnham: Ashgate, 2011.

———. "Dominion of Self and Natural Rights before Locke and After." In *Transformations in Medieval and Early-Modern Rights Discourse,* edited by Virpi Mäkinen and Petter Korkman, 173–203. Dordrecht: Springer, 2006.

————. *Foundations of the Conciliar Theory: The Contribution of the Medieval Canonists from Gratian to the Great Schism.* Cambridge: Cambridge University Press, 1955.

————. "Historical Roots of Modern Rights: Before Locke and After." *Ave Maria Law Review* 3 (2005): 23–43.

————. *The Idea of Natural Rights: Studies on Natural Rights, Natural Law, and Church Law, 1150–1625.* Atlanta, GA: Scholar Press, 1997.

————. "The Idea of Natural Rights: Origins and Persistence." *Northwestern Journal of International Human Rights* 2 (2004): 1–13.

————. *Liberty and Law: The Idea of Permissive Natural Law, 1100–1800.* Washington, DC: Catholic University of America Press, 2014.

————. "*Natura id est Deus*: A Case of Juristic Pantheism?" *Journal of the History of Ideas* 24 (1963): 307–22. Reprinted in *Church Law and Constitutional Thought in the Middle Ages*, chap. 7. London: Variorum, 1979.

————. "Natural Law and Natural Rights: Old Problems and Recent Approaches." *Review of Politics* 64 (2002): 389–406.

————. "Natural Rights in the Thirteenth Century: A *Quaestio* of Henry of Ghent." *Speculum* 67 (1992): 58–68.

————. "Origins of Natural Rights Language: Texts and Contexts, 1150–1250." *History of Political Thought* 10 (1989): 615–46. Reprinted in *Rights, Laws and Infallibility in Medieval Thought*, chap. 2. Aldershot: Variorum, 1997.

————. *Origins of Papal Infallibility, 1150–1350: A Study of the Concepts of Infallibility, Sovereignty and Tradition in the Middle Ages.* Second impression with a postscript. Leiden: Brill, 1988.

————. "Response to S. Adam Seagrave's 'How Old Are Modern Rights? On the Lockean Roots of Contemporary Human Rights Discourse.'" *Journal of the History of Ideas* 72 (2011): 461–68.

————. "Tuck on Rights: Some Medieval Problems." *History of Political Thought* 4 (1983): 429–41.

————. "Villey, Ockham, and the Origin of Individual Rights." In *The Weightier Matters of the Law: A Tribute to Harold J. Berman*, edited by John Witte, Frank S. Alexander, and Harold J. Berman, 1–31. Atlanta, GA: Scholars Press, 1988.

Troeltsch, Ernst. "The Idea of Natural Rights and Humanity." In Otto von Gierke, *Natural Law and the Theory of Society, 1500 to 1800: With a Lecture on the Ideas of Natural Law and Humanity by Ernst*

*Troeltch*, translated with an introduction by Ernest Barker, 201–22. Cambridge: Cambridge University Press, 1934; Boston: Beacon Press, 1957.

Tuck, Richard. *Natural Rights Theories: Their Origin and Development.* Cambridge: Cambridge University Press, 1979.

Vignaux, Paul. "Nominalism." In *Dictionnaire de théologie catholique*, 11:717–84. Paris: Letouzey et Ané, 1931.

———. *Nominalism au XIVe siècle.* Montreal: Institut d'Études Médiévales, 1948.

Villey, Michel. *Cours d'histoire de la philosophie du droit.* Paris: Dalloz, 1962.

———. *Le droit et les droits de l'homme.* Paris: Presses Universitaires de France, 1983.

———. *La formation de la pensée juridique moderne: Cours d'histoire de la philosophie du droit.* Paris: Ed. Montchretien, 1975.

———. "L'Idée du droit subjectif et les systèmes juridiques romains." *Revue historique de droit française et étranger* 24 (1946): 207–21.

———. "Le 'jus in re' du droit romain classique au droit moderne." In Michel Villey, *Conférence faites à l'Institut de Droit Romain en 1947*, 187–225. Paris: Institut de Droit Romain, 1950.

———. *Leçons d'histoire de la philosophie du droit.* Paris: Dalloz, 1957.

———. "Les origines de la notion de droit subjectif." *Archives de philosophie du droit* 2 (1953–54): 163–87.

———. *Précis de philosophie du droit.* 2 vols. Paris: Dalloz, 1977–78.

———. *Seize essais de philosophie du droit dont un sur la crise universitaire.* Paris: Dalloz, 1969.

———. "Suum jus cuique tribuere." In *Studi in onore di Pietro de Francisci*, 4 vols., 1:361–71. Milan: Giuffrè Editoré, 1956.

———. "La théologie de Thomas d'Aquin et la formation de l'État moderne." In *Théologie et droit dans la science politique de l'État moderne: Actes de la table ronde de Rome (12–14 novembre 1987)*, 31–49. Rome: École française de Rome, 1991.

Voegelin, Eric. *The New Science of Politics.* Chicago: University of Chicago Press, 1952.

Weigand, Rudolf. *Die Naturrechtslehre der Legisten und Dekretisten von Irnerius bis Accursius und von Gratian bis Johannes Teutonicus.* Munich: M. Hueber, 1967.

Westerman, Pauline C. *The Disintegration of Natural Law: Aquinas to Finnis.* Leiden: Brill, 1998.

Wilson, Daniel J. "Lovejoy's 'The Great Chain of Being' after Fifty Years." *Journal of the History of Ideas* 48 (1987): 187–206.

Zahora, Tomas. "Attendant to a Higher Judge: Competing Paradigms of Legal Practices in the Thought of Alexander Neckam (1157–1217)." *Journal of Religious History* 37 (2013): 494–509.

# INDEX

RICCARDO SACCENTI

is a scholar at the Fondazione per le Scienze Religiose

Giovanni XXIII in Bologna and teaches history of medieval

philosophy at the University of Bologna.